MEXICO

Corozal

Ambergris Caye

Orange Walk Town

Caye Caulker

Lamanai Altun Ha

St. Georges Caye

BELIZE CITY

Belmopan

English Caye

Actun Tunichil Muknal

MAYA MOUNTAINS

Tobacco Caye

Placencia

BELIZE (NOW)

GUATEMALA

Río Grande

Nuevo Laredo

SIERRA MADRE ORIENTAL

GULF OF MEXICO

Cancún

Mérida Chichén Itzá

Uxmal

YUCATAN (Chetumal)

MEXICO CITY

Ixtaccíhuatl

Hit by VW Beetle

Veracruz

Escárcega

Cholula

Becán

Popocatépetl

Cuernavaca

Oaxaca

Palenque

Tikal

BELIZE

GUATEMALA

Hondu

Fan belt breaks

Drive canal '51

EL SALVADOR

D0271694

TEQUILA OIL

Also by Hugh Thomson

The White Rock: An Exploration of the Inca Heartland

Cochineal Red: Travels through Ancient Peru

Nanda Devi: A Journey to the Last Sanctuary

TEQUILA OIL

GETTING LOST IN MEXICO

HUGH THOMSON

Weidenfeld & Nicolson
LONDON

First published in Great Britain in 2009
by Weidenfeld & Nicolson

1 3 5 7 9 10 8 6 4 2

A CIP catalogue record for this book
is available from the British Library.

ISBN: 978 0 297 85192 9

Typeset by Input Data Services Ltd, Bridgwater, Somerset

Printed in Great Britain by CPI Mackays, Chatham, Kent

Illustrations and endpapers © Emily Faccini 2009
Endpapers based on original maps by Hugh Thomson

The Orion Publishing Group's policy is to use papers that
are natural, renewable and recyclable products and made
from wood grown in sustainable forests. The logging and
manufacturing processes are expected to conform to
environmental regulations of the country of origin.

Weidenfeld & Nicolson

The Orion Publishing Group Ltd
Orion House
5 Upper Saint Martin's Lane
London, WC2H 9EA

An Hachette Livre UK Company

www.orionbooks.co.uk

Contents

INTRODUCTION

Most of the events described here took place a quarter of a century ago, when Mexico was a wilder and stranger place than it is today, although it still has many pockets of surprise and resistance to the modern world – as does neighbouring Belize, where my original journey ended, or was interrupted, and to which I recently returned to complete the last section of this book.

Those wanting a travel narrative in which the author is just a shadowy presence who never declares himself should look away now; this is an unashamedly personal story.

I should have quit you baby a long time ago,
I should have quit you pretty baby, then gone on to
Mexico.

HOWLING WOLF, 'KILLING FLOOR'

Runaway couple at the bar:
GIRL: 'Goddam, I love tequila. Why don't we go to
Mexico. You've been to Mexico, Brad. What's it
like?'
BRAD: 'Hot.'

Red Rock West (DIRECTOR JOHN DAHL, 1992)

Picaresque:
Main Entry: **ˈpi-ca-resque**
Pronunciation: ˌpi-k&-ˈresk, ˌpE-
Function: *adjective*
Etymology: Spanish *picaresco*, from *pícaro*: of or relating to rogues or rascals; *also*: of, relating to, suggesting, or being a type of fiction dealing with the episodic adventures of a usually roguish protagonist
<a *picaresque* novel>

PART ONE: THEN

I'm eighteen: I just don't know what I want.
Eighteen: I gotta get away, I gotta get out of this place.

ALICE COOPER, 'EIGHTEEN'

I 'm not sure why the stewardess did it. Maybe out of some perverse sense of humour, or my English accent, or because I had told her that I had never flown the Atlantic before. Or maybe one of my neighbours had complained about me.

'Come and sit in First Class, honey.'

I gaped.

'Come on, come and sit up front. There's a spare seat.'

My hesitation was from embarrassment as much as surprise. I looked a wreck: I hadn't been able to pack everything into my backpack, so had stuffed things into plastic bags at the last minute. What I couldn't fit in, I wore. So over a Kings Rd two-tone shirt and black drainpipe jeans, as approved by the punk orthodoxy of 1979, I had a set of survival army surplus fatigues from Millets.

That had been fine going to the airport through British weather. But this was an American flight and properly heated. Ever since take-off I had been discarding clothing. Over the ten hours or so it had taken to get to Houston, there had been so much spillage of one sort or another around me that my legs were now crouched up against my chest in the foetal position as we began the final leg down from the States to Mexico City.

'Shall I bring all my things, Gloria?' I knew she was called Gloria because of her Braniff badge. And despite her air-brushed American perfection (blonde, big breasts, big hair), I was enough miniatures away by now to have the courage to get personal.

'Why not?' said Gloria, smiling a smile that would have ignited galaxies.

Unsteadily I shuffled with my plastic bags down the length of the plane behind her, past the business section to the oasis of First Class. There were indeed only a few passengers dotted around. Gloria settled me into my new seat like some wonderful nurse. If there had been a hospital corner to the seat she would have tucked it in. I decided that I was in love with her. Wisely, I also decided this was not the time to tell her.

She helped me shuffle my plastic bags into some semblance of order. Miraculously they disappeared into the various and capacious overhead lockers. I surveyed my new quarters. It was like being on a yacht.

There was a Mexican in the armchair seat next to mine. He was well dressed in what I would later recognise as a trademark Mexico City businessman way: a 'sports' *chaqueta* in sombre charcoals, American slacks and a signet ring the size of a bull's testicle.

He leaned across, conspiratorially: 'Do you need another drink?' Although it was obvious to him that I had been drinking for some time before, the 'another' did not seem hostile.

'Have some of my champagne.' I did. Huge, tender steaks arrived. I was beginning to float. Life should always be like this, I felt. Life could always be like this.

Over whiskies, the businessman asked me what I knew of Mexico. 'Only what I've read,' I answered truthfully.

'*¿Cómo se llama?* What's your name?'

'Hugo.' I knew from trips to Spain that 'Hugh' was impossible for the hispanic tongue.

'Hugo, let me tell you something.' He paused, for effect. 'Let me tell you something. You're a young man [*jovencito*, literally 'small young man', but I let this ride]. Do you want to make some money here?'

'Yes,' I replied, cautiously.

The man looked at me with great sadness. 'In Mexico there is a lot of drugs and *narcotraficantes.*' He rolled the last word around with some savour.

Was it a character test or a sales proposition? I agreed as soberly as I could that drugs must certainly be a problem.

'Of course, you can make a lot of money travelling with drugs – but there is another way, an easier way.'

This was the sell. He leant forward, right across the armrests (a considerable distance) and grasped my shoulder.

'If you take a car from here', he gave a vague wave towards the Texas plains below us, 'and drive it right through Mexico down to Central America,' he made another gesture straight ahead, as if unravelling a carpet or bale of material, then paused: 'let me tell you my friend, someone will pay you good money for it. Someone will pay you very good money for it.'

I was being a little slow. 'Why?'

'Because of the dollar. *Nosotros no tenemos dolares. Ustedes, si. Así es.* We don't have dollars. You do. That's the way it is.

'But also because of taxes.' His eyes narrowed. 'We must pay import taxes. And not only taxes. If we drive a car through the borders, bamm!' He slapped the leather armrests between us. '¡*Nos muerdan*! They bite us!'

'I'm sorry?'

'*Nos muerdan*, they bite us, they take the little bite from us, the *mordida*, maybe as much as the whole car is worth. But you, a gringo, speaking fluent Spanish, you could do it.' He gave another vague, all-encompassing wave of the arms to suggest that in this world all is possible for those who ask for it. It was the first time in my life that anyone had suggested I might have the right qualifications for a job.

'Why take the car all the way to Central America?' My knowledge of geography was shaky, but it seemed perverse to travel right down to Belize or Guatemala, the first Central American countries going south. 'Why not just sell it in Mexico?'

'We have enough cars. But down there,' he smiled a little patronisingly, '*ellos pobrecitos no tienen nada de nada*, those poor little guys have nothing of nothing. You can sell them anything. A big American car, bought on the *mercado negro*, the black market – they'll think they own the planet. And because you'll have taken it through two borders, avoided two sets of import tax, the *policía* – you'll clean up.'

He settled back in his seat. By the time we crossed over into Mexico, he was asleep. I never learnt his name.

Under normal circumstances I would have forgotten the whole conversation. But these were not normal circumstances, as I sat there in the hallucinatory unreality of First Class, with Mexico coming up to meet me from the darkness below and pumped up with enough alcohol to have me flying anyway.

I was eighteen, far from home for almost the first time and with time to kill. It sounded the most sensible thing in the world.

I decided to do it.

CHIHUAHUA AND THE NORTH

O n one side of the Rio Grande, Ciudad Juárez, named after
Benito Juárez, the great nineteenth-century hero of the
young Mexican Republic; on the other side, El Paso, American
ever since the Mexicans handed it over to them, and just part of
the exorbitant price they had to pay the States after Independence –
not only Texas, but New Mexico and California as well.

I knew already about the enormous disparity between the
two: how you crossed from a squalid border town of fly-blown
llanterías, 'tyre shacks', and potholed streets to the hygienic malls
of American suburbia. What I also knew, more importantly, was
that after Detroit, El Paso was the next biggest 'used-car lot of
America'.

I had earned some money doing odd jobs translating in Mexico
City – not a lot, but enough, I hoped, to fly north and buy a
(very) cheap car. And I had an accomplice, an amiable Mexican
about my age called Fernando, whom I had met in a bar. I had

asked him for a cigarette, we had got talking and he'd said he would help me.

Ours was a fairly low-key campaign. Most of it involved hanging around bars and playing pool on the Mexican side of the border, as the minimum drinking age in Texas was twenty-one. Then around midday, after several beers and tequila chasers, we'd cross the border.

There were two sets of controls at the border bridge: one for long-term immigrants, and the other for people passing over for the day; a lot of American families had Mexican maids from Juárez. Once I'd crossed over for the first time by the main post and made my mark, I started using the *cotidiano*, the daily border control, explaining that I was seeing friends regularly in El Paso. Fernando had rich Mexican parents with an apartment there, so he had a regular pass anyway.

The Mexican guards noticed me because of my unusual passport. Apart from the stiffened imperial blue, they could not understand how it could last ten years; they were used to endlessly renewable short-term visas. When I first crossed, all the guards came over to check it out, their carbines clanking over their hips. 'This will last you for another ten years, to 1989? ¡*Hijo*!' Clearly they didn't relish having to inspect it on a daily basis for that long, so after the first day they would wave me through.

The American guards also got used to me. I was a distinctive figure: short hair, 'punk lite' clothes and my endlessly commented on English accent. One American guard, Rick, would ask me to say something each day and then laugh himself stupid. Although irritating, I made sure always to catch his eye at each crossing. I thought it might help when I eventually tried to cross in a car.

Using Fernando's family pick-up truck, we visited the various car lots and were laughed off the forecourts: 'You've got $500 to spend? Don't spend it all at once, boys.'

Then the small ads. Only one classified had anything so cheap. We turned up at a prosperous middle-class address, with a magnificent station wagon parked outside. My initial elation turned to worry when a policeman walked out. But he wasn't too concerned about my motives. Courteously he went over the car in detail for forty minutes – a spotless engine, legal tread tyres, no cigarette marks on the upholstery, a jack, full service history.

At the end he asked if we were interested.

Interested? I had the money all ready in dollar bills. He looked sadly at me. 'You do realise that it's $500 a *month* to the hire purchase company?'

And it was back to our daily routine. Although the hanging around went on a long time, I learnt a lot from Fernando. Indeed, the thing I really learnt from him was how to hang around. English youth culture never allowed for much – a bit of desultory mooching up and down the high street on wet afternoons or round the bus shelter on the village green, but no opportunities for serious time-wasting.

Fernando could hang around on an epic scale. I liked that. Also, I could beat him at pool. And he drank like a dying fish. All the time.

He could make a decision to play another game of pool or pinball seem like a day's work. Ciudad Juárez was not a place where much happened. It was a town full of breakers' yards, or '*yonkes*' as they called them, with cars so beaten-up that even I wouldn't touch them. Heavy trucks or Greyhound coaches – the Americans sold theirs to the Mexicans once they'd got old and fucked and failed the US safety regulations – would head straight down south from the border with their cargoes.

The bars were all holes in walls, run by men who looked as if they'd served with Pancho Villa. When we were not in *Billares Las Vegas*, 'Billiards Las Vegas style', we would try The Afro Bar, a seedy green building with enticing but false pictures of dancing girls on its outside walls. If unwise enough to eat there (and Fernando and I tried to make sure we did our midday run over the border in time to eat an El Paso hamburger), a shrivelled dish of *carne mollida* would emerge from behind a curtain.

Fernando was tall and lanky, with one constant catchphrase: '*Vamos a ver*. Let's see.'

'You think we'll find a car today?' '*Vamos a ver.*'

'Are you going to go back to college some time?' Fernando had a complicated history of seemingly interminable held-over courses. '*Vamos a ver.*'

'Why not get a job instead?' '*Vamos a ver.*'

He reacted with impassivity to my worries about whether there really was a black market for cars in Central America: '*Vamos a ver*', again. The first time he said this, I thought he meant to come with me. But then I realised it would have been too much effort. Only one thing animated him – whose turn it was to buy cigarettes. Partly because I didn't do it that often.

Sometimes I stayed at a cheap flophouse in Juárez. Or, when Fernando's parents were away, at their apartment in El Paso.

One day we were doing our afternoon cruise, trying to work out whose turn it was to buy the Marlboros, when we noticed a lot we'd never seen before, tucked away down an El Paso side street.

Right at the front was an electric blue Oldsmobile 98. Needless to say, I didn't recognise the model (all American cars looked alike to me – big), but it sounded good once I'd read what it was on the boot. I had hear of the junior version, the Oldsmobile 88, which was a celebrated rock'n'roll car – the 'Rocket 88' of the songs. And this was even more powerful. With added Cadillac fins. Walking around it, with all its chrome and its low-slung chassis, I knew what I'd realised as soon as I'd seen the $600 sign. It was the one.

Nobody seemed to be on the lot. We went back into the shack of an office. There were two men: an older guy with a big pot belly, his feet up on the desk drinking cans of Coors (years later I would see Orson Welles in *Touch of Evil* – 'I don't speak Mexican' – and recognise him immediately) and a younger, bigger man in a football shirt.

'What can we do for you all?' leered Orson Welles. 'The Oldsmobile?' He swung to his feet with surprising agility and led us back out.

'Power-steering. Air-conditioning. Rocket V8 engine.' He turned the key and pressed a button. We all listened respectfully as the windows purred down. 'Electric windows.'

I tried to remember what the policeman had said. 'Could I see the engine?'

'Of course, sir'. There was something funny about the way he said 'sir', but I let it ride. He opened it up. It looked liked . . . an engine.

'How about the boot?'

'The *what?*'

The big guy with football muscles laughed aloud this time. 'He means the trunk.'

'There doesn't appear to be a jack here.' I sounded prissy even to myself.

'Tell you what,' said Orson Welles, waving his hand expansively, 'buy this car and I'll throw in a jack for free.'

I kicked a tyre with my Chelsea boot. It seemed to be blown up.

'Can we, uh, talk about it in the office?'

'Sure we can talk about it in the *office*, but sir,' and he took me to one side and did a stage whisper that could have been heard in Juárez, 'what's with the Mexican?' He jerked a thumb at Fernando.

I drew myself up to my full 5 feet 10 inches and became very English. 'He's my friend.'

'Uh-huh. He's your friend.'

Fernando was looking stony-faced and saying nothing. This was because he had never got around to learning any English.

'Well fine, if he's your *friend*.' Back inside, the good ol' boy offered us some Coors from a luke-warm fridge.

I had remembered a question I ought to ask. 'How many miles has it done?'

'I believe', said Welles judiciously and looked down at his fingers as if the case was still under review, 'that she's done about 160,000. That's kilometres of course,' he said hastily. 'And this is a big-engined car, all of seven litres. They go on and on forever.' He made a motion as if unravelling the carpet – it was curiously similar to the one the Mexican on the plane had used.

It certainly was a very big engine. That much even I had noticed under the 'hood'.

He took the initiative. 'You see boys,' Fernando was now included in this cordial address as more Coors were handed around, 'this is a 1972 car. And what that does tell you?'

I was about to say, despite myself, 'old', before he answered his own question.

'It means it was made before those OPEC shitheads pulled their stunt, that's what. When all that oil crisis *sheet* hit the fan, they stopped making these gas-guzzlers anymore. Not that it uses that much gas of course,' he quickly added. 'But they started bringing in these Volkswagen Rabbits.' He said 'rabbit' with venom, the way the hunter does in Bugs Bunny. 'And all these pussy-eating *environmentalists*, [another word with a shotgun up against it] these environmentalists started to use catalysers and stuff. This car,' he said proudly, 'will run only on fully leaded gas.'

He paused. 'Do you two know the story about the lady who gets stopped for drunken driving?' It was clear he was going to tell us anyway. 'The cop pulls her over, gets out of the car, gets *her* out of the car.' Welles mimed all this elaborately as he did it. 'Then he unzips his pants. "Oooh" says the lady,' Welles's voice went squeaky, '"oooh, you want me to take the breathalyser?"'

His belly shook as he laughed. No one else did: the footballer because, presumably, he'd heard it before, Fernando because he couldn't understand it and I didn't because it was such a crap joke.

Undeterred, Welles carried on: 'How can you tell a Polish minesweeper?' I felt it would have been a Mexican minesweeper if Fernando hadn't been there. 'Because when he's sweeping, he goes like this,' and he mimed a man with his hands over his ears cautiously treading the ground. This time even Fernando laughed.

'Now do you intend, sir, to use the car in Mexico at all? Because if you do, then gas is cheap down there. In fact, so cheap they're pissing it away.' Given that I did indeed intend to use the car in Mexico in a very big way, this was good news.

Fernando surprised me by saying something: '¡*Hugo!*' He spoke with unusual urgency. '*Hombre, tienes que manejarlo.*'

He had a point. 'Can we give it a test drive?'

Welles looked at the young footballer. This was his demarcation zone. We all trooped back out to the narrow drag outside the showroom.

I got Fernando to do the actual driving, which consisted of a stately roll forward and back down the strip. I watched. When the footballer and Welles looked surprised, I just said (why hadn't I thought of this before?): 'He's a mechanic.'

Fernando came back. He looked like Buster Keaton after a fall. He whispered to me in Spanish that the car seemed to be fine. I whispered back to him to keep looking that way as we began final negotiations, which were made simpler by the fact that I really did only have $500 spending money in the world, particularly after drinking a fair amount away with Fernando. Even at the rock-bottom prices of Juárez bars, we had run up a formidable tab doing nothing.

They accepted $500. 'You sure drive a hard bargain,' said Orson, leering. 'Now I'm going to give you some temporary num-berplates [cardboard, with a number written on them] so you can take it with your insurance details and driving licence to the registration office. When you pay the registration fee, they'll hand you over your plates. The office is open until five o'clock and you should get registered right away, otherwise the cops will keep stopping you.'

I felt light-headed and happy. 'Want a cigarette?', as I offered almost our last.

'Not for me. Might stunt my growth,' said the footballer.

'Boys,' said Orson, 'I don't know where you're heading, but you've got yourself a mighty fine car to do it in.'

And we took it.

*

I had no intention of going to the registration office.

There were several reasons for this. For a start I had no insurance, nor did I intend to get any. I also had no money to pay any registration fee. I figured in Mexico no one was going to worry too much.

More seriously, I didn't have a driving licence of any sort. In fact not to put too fine a point on it (and it was something I had only half admitted to myself), I didn't know how to drive. Which was why I had let Fernando do the honours on the tarmac.

I thought it was time to break this last bit of news to Fernando. He took it calmly. '¡*Hombre*! ¡*No importa nada*! Man, that doesn't matter. No one in Mexico knows how to drive anyway.' He said this in his usual deadpan way. I thought he was joking.

Thank God the car was an automatic. 'All you do,' said Fernando, 'is engage the "D" the drive, and . . .' He made the same elegant unravelling of a carpet gesture that everyone else did, implying that the miles would fall away ahead of me.

I tried. It did indeed seem remarkably easy. I lit a cigarette with the car-lighter, turned on the radio. 'Jesus, I forgot to try the cassette machine.' I burrowed around in my precious plastic bag of tapes for some Elvis Costello: 'Oliver's army . . . is here to stay / and I would rather be anywhere else / than here today.'

¡*Chingada madre*!' said Fernando: 'What the fuck is that music?'

Crossing the border was a breeze. Rick waved me through without a glance. 'Have a nice day – or should I say "What a delightfully nice day we're having"?' He smirked. And I smiled to myself as we cruised on to the next controls at the Mexican end.

This was the bit I was worried about. I didn't want to have to bring the car into Mexico formally, which would have needed the correct papers, my passport stamped and, if I were to try to sell the car, a retrospective duty of 100 per cent (Mexican duty had been prohibitively high on imported – i.e. usually American – goods ever since 1947 when there had been a run on the peso).

A guard came over. I waved my passport at him like a good luck charm. *¿De quién es el carro?* Whose car?'

'We borrowed it from a friend – just visiting Juárez for the night.'

'*¿Por la noche?*, For the night?' The guard made an obscene hip movement that pushed his carbine against the car door. 'Fucky-fucky, uh,' he leered.

He waved us ahead.

I left Fernando at the first bar, as he wanted. We had a final couple of drinks: a celebratory *bandera*, 'flag', where you lined up shorts of red, white and green for the Mexican colours, sangrita, tequila and a lime chaser respectively. Then I said goodbye and left him settling into position by the pool table, waiting for somebody else to come along.

I bought a cheap plastic bottle of tequila at a liquor store. The old guy running it told me that what I really needed was a bottle mezcal because by the time I had driven all the way down 'there' (he made a gesture at the floor) to Belize, I'd be ready to eat the worm at the bottom of the bottle. His Spanish when he said, '*gusano*, worm', had the slow deliberate stress of the English spoken in the Southern States: 'gu-*san*-o', tasting the words before swallowing them.

Although it was getting dark, I drove on south in a sort of fever. After the long delay in getting hold of a car, I couldn't wait to begin the journey. The sickly lights of Juárez soon tailed away behind me and there was nothing ahead but the odd cactus silhouetted against the skyline, satisfactorily and exactly like a movie.

Every so often a Greyhound would veer up out of the night into the centre of the road and I would pull over. Discretion seemed the better part of valour. Someone had told me the

Mexican rule of the road when you came to what were usually single-lane bridges – the first car to flash its lights had right of way. Get it wrong and there would be no point in arguing about it later.

The driving was a breeze. Now there was nothing but highway, I could drive the car as fast as I liked. The speedometer wasn't working too well, but the power underneath me felt enormous. I headed for the dwindling horizon. I felt terrific. In fact I hadn't felt this wired up since Gloria took me through to First Class. Life from now on was going to be good.

I had another tape with me I played over and over again. I had bought it for just this occasion in El Paso:

> This is the story about Billy Joe and Bobby Sue
> Two young lovers with nothing better to do
> Than sit around the house and get high and watch the tube
> And here's what happened when they decided to cut loose:
>
> They headed down to ol' El Paso
> They swear they ran into a great big hassle
> Billy Joe shot a man while robbing his castle
> Bobby Sue took the money and ran.
>
> CHORUS: Go on take the money and run, ooh, ooh,
> go on take the money and run.

By the time I'd gone a few hours to this I was word-perfect. Steve Miller went on in the song to tell of Billy Mac, the detective from Texas who set out after the lovers to find out what had happened (the song neatly rhymed 'Texas' with 'what the facts is'). But it was the glorious moral of the ending that I really enjoyed:

. . . they got away.

They headed down south and they're still running today.

So go on, take the money and run, ooh, ooh,

go on take the money and run.

(repeat chorus three times)

I pulled down a side road and came to a tiny rail-crossing, where I stopped for the night. The back seat was easily big enough to sleep on. I had a last cigarette with my feet out of the window and watched as the fireflies clustered against the glass, curious about the dying embers at the end of the nicotine.

*

I was cold through and through when I woke up the next day. The railway ran in a straight line as far as the eye could see across the high Chihuahua plains. My little road was at right angles to it. There were a few vultures flapping around a dead coyote on the road, which cheered me up. I liked the idea of vultures and never understood why they were reviled. The difference between a vulture and a condor was one only of degree, and bad luck over a haircut. As scavengers they were just recycling. And looking at the vultures reminded me how hungry I was.

I got out a map. I had of course thought a little about how to make the journey while kicking my heels in El Paso, but the full enormity of it was just beginning to dawn on me.

Mexico was a surprisingly big country – surprisingly, because I had always thought of it as small in relation to the United States, and because the Mercator projection compressed it unnaturally compared to Canada above. According to my *South American Handbook*, which delighted in listing such facts, there were two million square kilometres of country ahead of me. And not only was it a big country, but comparatively empty, with a population the size of Britain's spread over ten times the land, a quarter of them crammed into Mexico City.

I could take the major routes, the highways like the *Panamericano*. But I hadn't come to Mexico to take the main routes and the Pan-American Highway. I had come to get lost.

Older cousins of mine and Sixties survivors had always talked to me as I was growing up of going east to India and 'finding themselves'. I wasn't too sure if they had succeeded in this or not; there didn't seem to have been much visible benefit. What I did know was that I violently didn't want to do the same. It was a hippy idea. If anything, I wanted to lose myself. And Mexico had always sounded the perfect place for that.

Every cowboy film I had seen as a kid always took on a new lease of life when the cowboys went 'south of the border'. Mexico was the place where they didn't have to let the other guy know they were there before shooting him.

So my plan was to do it the long way – to keep heading south, just like Billy Joe and Bobby Sue, but to see what happened and stop off whenever I felt like it, or, more importantly, whenever there was the chance of earning some money or having a free lunch. I needed badly to keep earning as I went, as I now had very little money left. And then, the scenario ran, I would sell my new, wonderful car for a small fortune when I finally arrived in Belize.

I set the milometer to zero and started off for the highway, where I found a shack selling *frijoles* and coffee. Driving on south, the desert in the dawn light was unexpectedly beautiful – the high chaparral covered with mesquite bushes, underpinned with verdant green creosote bushes and the little buttons of Spanish bayonet, the mountains cut against the horizon in the familiar tombstone blocks from the movies.

Travelling across the chaparral, I imagined how Pancho Villa's army had camped here during the Mexican Revolution, each man to his own mesquite bush, with a serape and strips of raw meat draped over the branches and a gun below; behind were the trains that bore the revolutionary army, 'pillars of fire by night and of black smoke by day', in the description of the remarkable American journalist who accompanied them, John Reed.

*

John Reed wrote young and died young: only twenty-six when he covered the Mexican Revolution – by far his best writing – and thirty-three when he died in Russia after the Bolshevik uprising. I had brought his *Insurgent Mexico* with me because it was as short and direct as a shot of tequila.

Reed travelled with Pancho Villa through this desert at the height of the General's powers, in 1913. Pancho Villa had been a regular backwoodsman bandit before being elevated to national importance by the convulsions of the Revolution. A supreme showman, able to dance all night and shoot a can at twenty paces, Villa created his own legend as a womaniser and brilliant horseman – but he could also plan every detail of his campaign down to the railway timetables, as Reed shrewdly noted.

The desert made for perfect railway country. Trains became central to the waging of the war, and not just for rapid troop deployment: the *locos locos*, 'mad trains', were packed with dynamite and sent headlong into enemy lines, creating havoc when they exploded.

John Reed described how Villa's army sometimes had to build

and repair the track as it advanced on the railway. On one troop train, Reed rode on the cowcatcher up front, which he shared with a woman baking tortillas and drying laundry by the steam of the boiler; on another occasion, he disturbed an army captain and his woman 'recreating' in the engine room.

Reed threw himself into combat with a gung-ho enthusiasm that made for great copy and plenty of enjoyable self-aggrandising. While accompanying Villa's troops, he relates how they implore him to go back from the front because the risks are too high; he doesn't, of course, and is embraced by the *compañeros*, who insist he beds down among them in the lice-infested blankets. Later, he excites jealousy among their women and is 'one hell of a fellow', gambling, drinking and setting a pose as the tough, gonzo journalist, a model for later twentieth-century war reporting from Hemingway to Michael Herr's Vietnam despatches:

> At noon we roped a steer and cut its throat. And because there was no time to build a fire, we ripped the meat from the carcass and ate it raw.

With Pancho Villa and his men, Reed created an image of Mexican wildness that was to play down the line to countless Westerns and Sergio Leone movies – of amoral brutality and a wayward sentimentality: singing *corridas* and sharing your last tortilla, while laughing at how the brains of your enemy had splattered the ground.

He recounts a terrific story of a general retreating with his army. The general has lost everything: his wife, his men, his weapons. Reed commiserates with him as he weeps, telling him that his men fought well. The general brushes this aside:

'It is not that,' he replied slowly, staring through tears at the pitiful company crawling down from the desert.

'I do not weep for them,' he said, twisting his hands together. 'This day I have lost all that is dear to me. They took my woman who was mine, and all my commission and all my papers, and all my money. But I am wrenched with grief when I think of my silver spurs inlaid with gold, which I bought only last year in Maipimi!' He turned away, overcome.

The mountains funnelled down either side of the chaparral as the Oldsmobile powered its way south and the land became more fertile: small green oaks started to show up against the landscape, with a few cotton plantations and cattle ranches. The ranch houses were tantalising oases at the end of long dirt tracks, with their cow-horn gates giving right onto the highway, and often a windmill and a grove of trees surrounding the low terracotta house with its water cistern on the roof.

As I drove, the long straight road across the high plains made me notice something odd about the car: if you took your hands off the wheel and left it to its own devices, it veered violently off to one side. It didn't feel right. I resolved to fix it when I got to Chihuahua.

*

Chihuahua (City) was the capital of Chihuahua (State). I wanted to send a letter back home, just to get in that 'Chihuahua, Chihuahua' at the top.

It was a sedate town. Fernando had told me about it – full of rich cattle families, like his, and Americanised, with wide streets,

Colonel Sanders, a 'Robin Hood Inn' and even a multi-storey car park.

It was in the multi-storey car park that I had a bad moment. Designed, like all car parks, to accommodate as many as cars as possible, the sweep-space around each corner as you went up a floor was tiny. After having managed the couple of hundred miles from the border, I had relaxed into thinking I knew what I was doing. But I kept misjudging the turns, stalling and juddering to a halt. I finally found a space. It looked tight. It was tight and no one had told me how difficult parking was. I scraped the car next to mine badly with my bumper, right down its length.

It didn't seem a good idea to stay. I backed out and careered off down again to the exit. This time I really started catching things – walls, pick-up trucks – as I turned down each level. The parked cars had a lot of things that stuck out. So did my Oldsmobile. It made a nasty pinging noise each time we hit something.

I tried to compose myself with the attendant, who had moments before seen me come in cheerful, smoking and feeling like James Dean at the start of a brand-new day. 'Forgot something,' I muttered as I went off at speed.

A friendly mechanic at a little backstreet *taller*, 'workshop', helped me assess the damage. The car had different-coloured streaks of paint on it from all the vehicles I'd hit. 'Nothing a little paste won't fix,' the mechanic muttered cheerfully. He had the improbable name of, El Ruso, 'the Russian'. When I told him what I was doing, he advised against bothering to paint over the filler until I got to Mexico City. 'You'll get plenty more dents before then.' El Ruso fixed the wheel alignment, so the car wouldn't wander from the straight and true so much. I had broken the back assembly of lights on one side of the car – El Ruso suggested just putting some reflective tape over it.

'What about the indicator?' I asked.

He laughed. ¡*Hombre*! Safer not to use it anyway.'

I went to the Pancho Villa Museum. It had an inappropriate setting in a quiet suburb, given that Pancho Villa was the least polite of all the Mexican revolutionaries. While his contemporary Emiliano Zapata at least had some revolutionary if simple ideals, with his famous slogan '*Pan y Libertad*, Bread and Liberty', Pancho Villa was in it more for the kicks – less Robin Hood than Ronnie Biggs.

It might seem odd that Pancho Villa should have ignited the Revolution here in Chihuahua, the state furthest to the north from Mexico City, but there were good reasons: this was an area with a long historical resistance to the idea of the big *haciendas*, the old estates that kept their workers in perpetual bondage to the company store.

Throughout the nineteenth-century, Apache raids from the north had made it a lawless land. So the Mexican government had withdrawn the federal army and instead armed local communities, creating a tradition of truculent border-state independence that Villa was later to exploit. And because they were so close to the States, bandits could always slip over the border if they needed to, as Villa and others frequently did during the early years of the Revolution: at one point he 'invaded' Mexico from El Paso with just four men; within months he had won the state of Chihuahua back.

From John Reed's writing, I had an image of him careering over the railways of northern Mexico, his *Dorados*, the 'Golden Ones', spilling out of the roofs and windows of carriages as they went on the rampage. On those campaigns when he had to retreat, his men ripped up the train lines behind them as they went so that no one could follow, like a Tom and Jerry cartoon.

In later years, after a series of campaigns against just about every other revolutionary leader apart from Zapata, he had the supreme nerve to 'invade' the States in 1916 – the last person to have done so. Only eighteen Americans died during his night raid on New Mexico, but the States overreacted. Woodrow Wilson, coming up for re-election, launched the Pershing Raid with thousands of men in retaliation and chased Villa down to the hills of the Sierra Madre.

I was the only visitor in the out-of-the-way museum. Mexicans, it appeared from the dusty visitors' book, were no longer that interested in Pancho Villa or the Revolution. The rest of the world had long been indifferent, despite the fact that the decade of the Mexican Revolution from 1910 to 1920 had a lasting influence in Latin America, anticipated the Bolshevik uprising – not for nothing did Trotsky choose to flee to Mexico – and left a million dead.

There was a photo hanging on the wall of Pancho Villa together with General Pershing, taken at a meeting on the border a few years before relations turned sour. Villa was smiling and wearing a jaunty little bow tie. Pershing was laughing out loud. A few years later, Pershing would be trying to hunt Villa down like a rat.

It was an oddly satisfying photograph. There was a joviality about the group, in their hats and moustaches, that reminded me of *Butch Cassidy and the Sundance Kid*. Behind Villa and Pershing, in their row of supporters, was the young face of an American Army lieutenant, George Patton. And beside Villa stood Obregón, his revolutionary colleague, who was later to betray Villa and condone his assassination in 1923.

One striking detail about the photo was that while Pershing and Obregón were wearing starched uniforms, as befitted military men, Pancho Villa, standing between them and dominating the picture, sported a dishevelled safari jacket, with one pocket flap in, the other out. Aside from a medal dangling casually like a pocket watch from his waist, he could have been a farmer down from the hills. As indeed he was.

There was one extraordinary attraction to the museum. It was presided over by Pancho Villa's eighty-seven-year-old widow, Doña Luz. This was a little like finding Lenin's widow tending his mausoleum in Moscow, given that the Mexican Revolution pre-dated the Bolshevik. But then as Villa had cheerfully married a great many women, there was an odds-on chance that one of them would have survived to a venerable age.

Doña Luz was a huge, stone-faced woman, who looked up from the TV at me as if I were a fly. I tried to hold her gaze. 'Go and look at the car,' she barked at me, as an order. I had passed an old car outside without much of a glance. Now I saw that it was pockmarked with bullet holes. A card said that it was the car in which Villa had been assassinated.

I came back to her. An awkward pause in the conversation was broken when Doña Luz reached into a bag for a crumpled photo of herself holding one of Pancho Villa's shotguns; a collection of the guns lined the walls. She signed it for me with the scrawny, wavering handwriting of a six-year-old and turned back to her interminable Mexican soap opera.

Pancho Villa was popular back in England, I told her. This was flattery. I doubted if any of my friends had ever heard of him except as a joke Mexican name, like Speedy Gonsalez. Hadn't Yul Brynner played him in a movie once?

In fact, Villa had played himself in a movie once. In one of the most extraordinary contracts ever signed in Hollywood, the principal man agreed that for *The Life of General Villa* in 1914, he would fight all his coming battles during daylight hours for the cameraman. A rider was added that he would also move any executions from dawn to a few hours later when the light was better; quite what the condemned prisoners made of these few hours of reprieve is not recorded.

I asked Doña Luz what had happened when Villa met up with Zapata, his famous revolutionary counterpart from the south, later that same year of 1914. The two of them had entered Mexico City in triumph and put their boots on the table of government for a brief moment. Then the real operators, like Obregón, had taken over.

Doña Luz had stayed behind in Chihuahua, so had not met Zapata. But she did tell me a remarkable story about how Villa had rounded up all the orphans sleeping in the streets of Mexico City – and shipped them back to Doña Luz to look after: 'He sent me a telegram saying "300 orphans arriving on next train".' She had found them all homes, and was proud of it: while many of the orphans had absconded to the streets again, others had stayed, found jobs and a few were still alive and living in Chihuahua: her *niños*, her 'children', as she still described them.

The conversation was getting more interesting and she turned the TV off. With some hesitation, I asked her about a key incident that had decided Villa's fate. For a brief moment, Villa had Obregón in his power and with foresight knew that if he didn't kill him, Obregón would both betray the Revolution and assassinate Villa himself. But Doña Luz had protested that as Obregón was in their house, he was a guest, and to kill him would break Mexican laws of hospitality. So Villa compromised, sending Obregón away by train and asking his generals to murder him on the journey. They either failed or refused, and Obregón survived to fulfil both Villa's prophesies.

'All these years later, I'm still surprised that El General Francisco

Villa [she never called him Pancho] listened to me. What I said, I said quickly and without thinking.' She paused and seemed to lapse into deep thought.

Stacked on the table in front of Doña Luz were copies of her own recent autobiography, *Pancho Villa en la Intimidad* ('An Intimate Portrait of Pancho Villa'). They had been printed privately, on cheap paper. I bought one and she signed my copy with a flourish: '*Hugo, con todo cariño.* To Hugh, with fond regard.'

The book dealt frankly with Villa's outrageous serial polygamy; most biographers were unsure as to how many wives he had 'married' in false ceremonies. At one point Doña Luz had arrived in Chihuahua to find a rival 'wife' had taken over her house. But I knew from other accounts that Luz had been a central figure in Pancho Villa's life. He had married her at the start of the Revolution, in 1911, although she must have had misgivings when Villa, asked if he wanted the customary confession before the wedding, declined as he said it would take too long.

One biographer estimated that Villa had a dozen such wives, and got his men to destroy the marriage certificates secretly after each ceremony. Doña Luz had somehow stayed with him through the thick and often thin of the war-torn decade that followed, nobly taking in his children from other liaisons, even when one of her own daughters was poisoned by a rival wife.

It must have been an unruly household. At one point, she told me, Doña Luz discovered that the older children had soaked one of the younger ones with petrol and were about to burn him. Her response? To stop their pocket money and Sunday cinema outings.

She had also battled for Villa's reputation over the more than fifty years since his death, during which time she had lived on the pension awarded her by Obregón in gratitude for having saved his own life the decade before. One of Villa's assassins had just published a book called, baldly, *Yo Maté a Pancho Villa* ('I Killed Pancho Villa'). The museum did not stock it and Doña Luz was indignant at its publication: '¡*Que sinvergüenza*! How shameless!'

As I left, she gave me a final bit of advice: '*Joven*, young man, remember one thing – during his entire life, El General Francisco Villa never drank or gambled. *En su vida*, in his entire life.' It was a worrying thought. I didn't say this to her, but if Pancho Villa could kill and ravage quite as much as he did when stone-cold sober, what would he have been like with a drink inside him?

Nor was it quite true. For in his very last years, after he had ejected Doña Luz from his home for a younger model, he was known to have turned to drink. Like most of Pancho Villa's life, it ran like a country and western song.

＊

I was sleeping in the car. To be honest, I had hardly stepped out of it. This wasn't just to save money. I was in love with the thing, with its radio and its chrome and the sheer excess of its size. I could happily sit at an interchange, with the air-conditioning on, watching the Mexican college girls coming home each day for lunch, and still be sitting in the car when they returned later at four in the afternoon. The older eighteen-year-old ones had the tall, slim build of the northern Mexicans, dark hair with checked blue dresses and little white socks. They were laughing and flashing their bright white teeth in the afternoon sunshine.

Then I bumped into Fernando again, in a bar. He had come down from the border because he 'got bored'. I couldn't quite imagine this. Fernando had struck me as a man who could put a Beckett hero to shame with his capacity for endless lassitude.

His arrival meant I could now move into his parents' house and have a shower. His father, always referred to as 'El Licenciado', literally 'the qualified one', because he had a degree, was a quiet man with a moustache. His mother was also quiet. Indeed the whole family – Fernando had brothers and sisters – were unusually quiet, like him. After a few days I discovered why.

Fernando's mother had a large glass jar filled with coloured capsules on the breakfast table. In an American home (and like most of Chihuahua, this was carefully styled to look like an American home) it would have been filled with cookies. She had tranquillisers in there – serious ones like Valium and Mogadon, which I knew from my own juvenile escapades. At the first sign of what she considered overactivity by any of her children, like making a joke, she would make them take one. At the least, they would have one a day – '*medicina*' as she called it, or 'mother's little helper' as I did.

There was only so much I could take of a family that were permanently tranquillised and living on take-out pizza. I begged Fernando to create a diversion. We decided to head off to a ranch he knew, with some friends. He was a little vague about it, as riding was not his thing. But I was insistent, as the vision of those 'oasis ranches' I had seen on my drive south had stayed with me.

The planning took a considerable time. 'Planning' was perhaps too ambitious a word for anything Fernando did. But eventually we set off, the Oldsmobile riding low with five people, their luggage, six-packs and whisky. At the last moment one of the boys called El Grifo, 'Dopehead', brought a tent in case there weren't enough beds at the ranch. I had a sleeping bag.

We had been drinking heavily before we headed off and I had a Troggs tape I played at full volume. It was not long before the Mexicans were making the inside of the car shake with a version of 'Wild Thing'; they were weak on the verses, but terrific when it came to the chorus: '*Wi-ild* thing / you-er make my heart *si-ing.*'

We headed along dirt tracks that became increasingly dustier and more potholed. Fernando and El Grifo got me to roll the car from side to side to avoid the holes, but I could tell it wasn't doing the undercarriage of the car much good. Every so often, we would come to fords over dry river beds. 'What happens if it rains?' I'd ask.

They laughed. 'You can't cross of course. But it only rains once or twice a year anyway, and in the rainy season.'

As they said this we saw clouds coming up over the horizon. Within the hour, it had started to rain. Not effete British rain, but sleet rain, which even at its fastest wipe-setting the Oldsmobile couldn't keep from flooding the windscreen. I switched the tape off and tried to navigate along what was becoming a mud-slide. We just made the next crossing, although the water swirled up the sides of the car. By the time we got to the one after that, it was hopeless.

'How far are we from the ranch?' I asked.

Fernando shrugged. '*No sé – no puede estar tan lejos.* I don't know – it can't be that far.' This meant we still had a long way to go.

El Grifo rolled another joint. 'Not much we can do then'.

'What about the tent?' suggested someone. In retrospect this was not a good idea. But we had already drunk our way through quite a few of the six-packs and our judgement was, at best, cloudy.

By the time the tent was up, we were extremely wet. Three of us pitched into the tent. The others stayed in the car. Sodden and exhausted, clutching a virgin bottle of El Licenciado's Ballantines whisky, I tried to get some sleep. At some point in the middle of the night it stopped raining. It was around then that El Grifo started to vomit.

Not usually an early riser, I ducked my head out of the tent as soon as I could, nursing a deep, metallic hangover and tried to focus on the world. The first thing that came into proper definition was a large fuzzy shape rearing up towards me with its two front legs. I was directly at eye level with it. It could have been my brain come back to get me.

I backed off and zipped the tent up. Through the air vent at the top, Fernando and I watched the spider stalk off in a proprietorial way to a nearby hillock. Fernando confirmed that it was a tarantula, although he had only ever seen pictures of them. I kidded him about this. 'How can you be a Mexican and never have seen a tarantula?'

'*Es cosa de campo*,' he said dismissively, 'it's a country thing.'

I had already come across Fernando's disdain for all things outside the city. It was with considerable effort that I had got him out to the ranch at all.

Giving a wide berth to the tarantula, which sat observing us from afar like some malign frog, we threw the vomit-soaked tent into its bag and joined up with our *compadres* in the car. They seemed cheerful. They had kept the engine running for a while the night before while drinking and smoking dope. In the process they had also managed to leave the headlights on, run the battery down and now the car wouldn't start.

There was no human habitation visible on the horizon, but a file of twelve-year-old boys emerged from behind a rock. They were wearing Boy Scout uniforms. It was a strange moment, like a Buñuel movie. My companions were unmoved by its oddity. Indeed the whole concept of strangeness, in the English, ironic way ('what a strange thing to happen'), seemed to mean nothing in Mexico. Things happened.

The Boy Scouts had apparently been camping close by. Even

better, they offered us some breakfast, which they cooked meticu-
lously on collapsible stoves. I managed to ask politely about the
Baden-Powell movement, which I was glad to hear was flourishing
in Chihuahua. One of them asked if I had ever been a Boy Scout
myself. I didn't like to tell them that I hadn't made the grade.

Some *campesinos* came by in a truck and helped get the Oldsmobile started with jump-leads. We limped on towards the ranch,
Peñas Azules. When we got there, we found the horses had all
been moved on to another ranch, Rancho Grande. At least we
could have a wash and some beans. A pick-up was heading to
Chihuahua, and Fernando and his friends decided they'd catch a
lift back. The wet night had put them off the whole enterprise.

I made my own way over to Rancho Grande, asking for directions as I went. Asking for directions was made difficult in
Mexico because it was considered rude not to give them even
when the person doing so didn't know the way. The usual response
was '*derecho, derecho*', effectively 'just straight ahead, follow your
nose', accompanied by a hand gesture forward. It was the gesture
that was crucial. If the hand should waver at all in the pointing,
should become too all-inclusive or shiver a bit as if the wind were
moving, it was an infallible sign that the teller had not the slightest
idea of where you wanted to go.

I only learnt this as I went along and so the journey to the other
ranch was circuitous. Far from being large, Rancho Grande when
I got there was a small building with just one stocky cattleman
running it, Eleuterio. He lived there with his wife and small
daughter.

I was concerned about horse riding, which, like driving a car,
I had never done before; but the saddles were as big as armchairs
and falling off them was almost impossible. Eleuterio taught me
to ride the Mexican way by coming up behind me as I cantered

genteelly along and trying to scare my horse: it would then take off across the horizon as I clung on.

A day of this and I was hooked. I asked Eleuterio if I could stay for a while.

So began a very happy period. Eleuterio was only too glad to have someone around to help. We spent eight hours a day in the saddle. By the third day I was so stiff in the evening, I couldn't sit down to eat, much to his amusement. He laughed even harder the following day when I tried to lasso a steer by the neck and was left with a rope burn that peeled half my hand away. '¡*Coño, no haces así!*' he shouted, 'Don't do it like that, you cunt! [a more affectionate word when used in Spanish] Grab them by the legs.'

We would ride up into the hills to fix a broken water pump, or, quite often, seem to be riding around just for the hell of it, although this was never quite how Eleuterio explained it to his quiet wife, who gave us black beans and tortillas washed down with black coffee. The days when there really was nothing much to do were marked with a siesta.

The days turned into weeks. I became a literal redneck as my skin blistered and cracked in the sun. Looking in the mirror one day, I was surprised how healthy I seemed. The only drink I had with me was the bottle of Ballantines, which I eked out slowly with Eleuterio in the evenings when we sat out on the veranda under the stars smoking and getting philosophical. When we finished the whisky, he brought out some old *reposado* tequila.

Eleuterio was not a happy man. He was bored rigid by a life that appeared so idyllic to me that I could contemplate staying forever. He asked me about England and whether there was a wet season:

'You mean it's green all the time?'

'Yes. Because it's wet all the time.'

Some evenings I would feel guilty of my abandonment of the Oldsmobile and take it for a twilight cruise up and down the lane, watching the fireflies cluster again to the headlamps and catching strange Tex-Mex country and western stations on the radio dial.

I had books with me too, which I could finally get round to reading, by some of the writers who had headed to Mexico in search of lawless roads and a supposed lack of any moral code: D. H. Lawrence, Evelyn Waugh, Aldous Huxley, Malcolm Lowry and Graham Greene – although they were from such a different era. For a younger voice, I had *The Catcher in the Rye*; also the Carlos Castaneda tales of Don Juan and his shamanic powers. I had already asked Fernando about the local availability of peyote. He had looked at me as if I were out of my mind. '*Cosa de indios,*' he muttered disparagingly, 'An Indian thing.'

I thought about just staying and forgetting the whole car-running business. Maybe I could take the Oldsmobile back up to Orson Welles in El Paso, throw myself on his (probably limited) supplies of mercy, and return here to live out my cowboy fantasies with Eleuterio.

What made it all so appealing was that it was like *The Virginian*. I would play the theme music in my head as Eleuterio and I picked our way across some dried-up river bed. I had expected there to be some difference – for the reality to be more muted than the Hollywood version.

But a certain stubbornness took over. Early one morning I rolled up the sleeping bag, had my last coffee with the family and headed on south. I left Eleuterio with a Bob Dylan tape he said reminded him of Hank Williams. I liked to think of him sitting out on the veranda and listening to 'All Along the Watchtower'.

DURANGO BADLANDS

T he cop moved in slow motion. He leaned over the windscreen and gave me the once-over. Years later I saw *Psycho* and felt for Janet Leigh when the motorcycle cop stopped her as she headed off for the motel with all the money – a certain choreography, the deliberation with which he leant over, the dark glasses, the long pause. 'OK, we better go inside and talk about this.'

Although I'd tried to take minor roads heading south, I'd run into a roadblock just on the outskirts of Hidalgo del Parral, a lumber and mining town on the edge of the Sierra Madre. 'Inside' meant sitting down at the only table in a shack opposite where a *viejecita*, 'little old lady', was making coffee. I tried to present my case, which was mainly one of wondering naivety ('Do I need to have insurance?' etc.).

He looked at me in disbelief: '*Coño*, you cunt, *tienes huevos*, you've got some balls.' This seemed a contradiction in terms, but it was not the moment to point it out. 'No driving licence, registration or insurance. Not even a fucking numberplate!' I had taken the cardboard plate off as I thought it would blow away.

'I may have to impound your car.' He leant forward: 'Tell me something – do you want a job?'

I couldn't quite believe what he was saying. Surely my misdemeanours hadn't just earned me an honorary place in the Mexican police squad, like the old jokes about getting into Military Intelligence by failing the entrance test?

'A job. At the sawmill on the other side of town. The foreman told me they're looking for a translator at the moment. Your Spanish is pretty good.'

'Uh, what about the car?'

'Like I say I'm temporarily impounding it.' He gave me various stamped official forms to study. 'There is your *documentación*, documentary proof'. It was about the only documentation I had that showed the car existed. I studied it with curiosity. I had always assumed that Mexicans didn't care about paperwork, that they would be too easy-going to bother. Nothing could be further from the truth. Just buying a pencil from a stationers involved the preparation of forms in triplicate.

'Maybe,' the policeman gave an indecipherable smile, 'I'll give it back to you later.' I had to leave the car behind the police station in town. Locking whatever I could in the trunk (he let me keep the key), I carried off essential supplies – my tapes, diary and a few clothes – in my backpack and some plastic bags.

Hidalgo del Parral was a real cowboy town, unlike Chihuahua. The air was raw and clean, with mountains in the distance. A Madonna the size of a barn was tacked up above the church. Ford 100 Custom pick-ups passed by full of ranchers: many had Tarahumara Indian blood in them, with a lean, burnt look; the Tarahumara were celebrated long-distance runners. The main stores in what was the only street in the place had rows of cowboy boots in the window, elaborately stitched affairs with snakeskin or armadillo sections added to the basic brown leather. One shop was called Tarahumara Boot's. I liked the apostrophe.

Heels were categorised by angle of rake numerically, from one to eleven – a 'one' was a relatively modest affair, like a normal shoe; by 'eleven' the heel was virtually a stiletto, high and cutting right back to the sole. They looked impossible to walk on. I passed a couple of cowboys on the way to the sawmill, big guys in lumber-shirts and ten-gallon hats, who somewhat compromised the effect by mincing along in these high-heeled boots. Real men clearly went for the size elevens.

I made myself known at the sawmill. While waiting for the foreman to arrive, I watched a sawyer throwing 16-foot logs around with his machine as if they were matchsticks, slicing them down with a circular saw, and sending the slivers down rollers to be edged, sorted and graded.

Still in shock from losing my car, I was overwhelmed by it all: the noise of the machines, the saw sending up a fine spray of wood dust that the light caught, the penetrating smell of formaldehyde. The sawyer was a dark Tarahumara Indian. He wore thigh-high rubber boots to guard against the spray of wet chippings. After a while he changed the blade, casually flipping the circle-ribbon of steel onto the workhouse floor, where it writhed and flexed itself before settling back into passivity like a dying fish.

Zack, the foreman, was from Texas. His conversational opener was to tell me how the day before a pipe had burst in the methanol plant, leaving one of his men with 80 per cent burns. Zack had been there for years, so didn't need any help understanding Spanish; the translator was needed for a sister-plant right out in the Western Sierra Madre, which a Canadian lumber expert was due to visit.

He couldn't find anyone who would go there because it was so remote. When I explained that I didn't have my own transport – although I didn't mention why – he laughed: 'The only way into Tahonas is to fly.'

The money sounded good and there seemed a certain inevitability about the whole situation. Within hours I was the only passenger in a Cessna flying deep over the Sierra Madre.

This was the bandit country that Pancho Villa had headed into when on the run from the Americans. I could see how it was they never caught him. Forested mountains, with deep ravines cut into them, rippled away forever. The pilot pointed out some of the small airstrips perched in odd positions on the hills: one had a bend in the middle and ended at a cliff-top.

'Dope-runners,' explained the pilot. Up until a few years before, this had been the main growing area for running marijuana up to the border. Then the Americans had linked up with the *federales* to spray the home-grown plantations from the air in the brilliantly code-named 'Operation Condor'. Now the government had tried to set up small local cooperatives, called '*ejidos*', to supply the big sawmills with timber, as a replacement crop.

The pilot sighed sadly. The farmers had gone from earning 500 pesos a day growing dope to 120 a day providing timber – which was in any case harder work. It was clear what he thought of this. Moments later, he took me over a couple of clearings in the forest he said were still being used to grow marijuana. This made sense of the strange scene at the airstrip when soldiers had searched me before I got on the plane. It had been nothing excessive – no intimate body cavities – but had taken me aback.

Ed MacDonald was the Canadian lumber expert waiting for me at the other end. Aged sixty-eight, with a white floppy hat, he wasn't quite what I was expecting. But then I probably wasn't quite what he had expected either.

I thought it better to reveal at once my total ignorance of lumber. He gave me a running lecture as we drove. The tall ponderosa pines we passed, for instance, were prized because they didn't taper and were self-pruning for the first hundred feet, so left no wood knots. Ed himself had worked in the timber business since he was a boy of fourteen in British Columbia.

Tahonas turned out to be a collection of small log huts sheltering below a rise. At over 7,000 ft, it got fiercely cold at nights. Ed had only arrived the day before and already had some complaints about the accommodation, an old schoolroom with a cracked toilet, and the food, which was the usual *norteño* diet of refried beans, tortillas, black coffee and Coca-Cola. The coke was the only ingredient that was consistently warm.

We drove or flew to the small local sawmills. The flying was hard work. The pilot would cross himself before take-off and Ed held forth at length about how our plane was 'a pile of crap that would probably fall apart on landing'.

The Tarahumara rarely show surprise at anything, but the sudden appearance at their sawmills of an elderly red-faced man in a white floppy hat with a spiky-haired eighteen-year-old assist-ant in Chelsea boots did prompt a certain startled impassivity.

Ed was being paid to advise them on possible improvements and he didn't hold back. Translating his red-blooded lumberman's comments to a group of *ejido* workers lined up beside their foreman needed the diplomatic skills of a Chinese courtier. I would try to turn what he said ('That's a crap way of working') into the very correct Castilian Spanish always used by the Mexicans at such meetings ('There may be other ways of working that are more beneficial to the enterprise').

Despite his comments, Ed had a grudging respect for the way the Tarahumara were doing things – and he was not a man who respected people easily. He had virulent opinions, for instance, on black immigrants to Britain, who in his view were only surpassed in laziness and mendacity by French Canadians.

The local foreman at Tahonas was called Enrique, a big jovial man who looked like the Park Ranger in *Yogi Bear*. Enrique was a fanatical radio buff, always listening to his short-wave set. He would sometimes report back to us from the outside world; he once picked up a speech by the newly elected Mrs Thatcher.

One day even Ed was bored by doing nothing but talk about trees, so we headed off in Enrique's pick-up for a diversion. Enrique was in a state of high excitement. The mango season had begun and we would drive down into one of the deep canyons to find some.

After our constant flatulent diet of beans, Ed and I were more than ready for this. I hadn't seen a fruit of any description in months. Nor had I ever eaten a fresh mango before; in Britain in the 1970s, an avocado was considered exotic – a mango was off the map.

The road was atrocious. Enrique had a theory about the bumps – that you should take them slowly going up, then very fast going down. The effect was like being on an erratic fairground whirligig. Combined with the midday heat, Ed MacDonald started to turn green.

We passed a 10,000-foot mountain called the Cerro de Mohinora, before plunging into the ravine the other side that led to our mango valley. The road was so bad, I had to stand on the back of the open pick-up truck to weigh us down over the bumps, bracing myself against the cabin each time Enrique did his slam-dance technique on the accelerator pedal.

The Apache pines were back-lit by the sun like fibre optic lamps, with their long needles translucent. As we descended, the pines started to give way to oak forests – 'good for parquet flooring,' shouted Ed. He had already told me that a bewildering profusion of over 300 types of oak grew in the Sierra Madre: the coolness of the silver-leaved and blue oaks stood out against the green of the willow oaks. Sometimes, we would disturb a group of Mexican jays foraging for acorns amongst them, who would rise up in a cacophony of shrieking as the pick-up passed.

The oaks, juniper and hackberry thickets started to thin down to more tropical vegetation: organ pipe cacti and ceiba trees with their burst cotton-bud pods. There were small settlements of Tarahumara who had planted groves of oranges and bananas, with a few goats scratching around the wooden cabins.

By the time we finally reached Dolores at the bottom of the valley, we had dropped several thousand feet and the ravine was trapping the midday heat. Ed carried a thermometer with him that registered 100 degrees; he also carried a compass and emergency first aid kit with him at all times, and had been impressed when I passed on as a joke the *South American Handbook*'s suggestion of always travelling with a spare rubber bath plug. After a five-hour drive, he was suffering badly and I was concerned. Apart from anything else, he was my meal ticket.

We sheltered in a cool whitewashed house at the centre of Dolores. The villagers here seemed unlike the Tarahumara I was used to from the sawmills – smaller, fairer and with wry, shrewd faces; they had more European blood. Enrique told me that a party of French settlers had come here during the brief interregnum of Maximilian in the nineteenth century, the absurdly tragic attempt by Napoleon III to make his nephew emperor of the country, which ended in the firing squad for Maximilian. I liked to think of French settlers making their way into the Sierra Madre, their wagons filled with the heavy furniture of the period, before settling here because of the opportunities for mango production.

There was indeed an old French nineteenth-century sideboard in the room, with a lace-covered Virgin de Guadalupe on it. As we recovered from the heat, sipping cool lemonades, Ed told me an odd story about his experiences in the war. He had been part of the Allied forces that took Berchtesgaden. While the other troops had been looting the house for the valuables they supposed Hitler had left behind (Ed gave a dismissive wave of the hand for the vanities of human folly), he himself had discovered a remarkably fine walnut tree in the garden. 'Say what you like about Hitler, but he knew about trees.' He had cut off a bough and made a chessboard from it when he got back to Canada. 'Always remember, Hugh, that walnut is the finest of all the hardwoods. It will last for a thousand years. Unlike the Reich.'

Enrique had gone to find the mangoes. They weren't ripe yet, but the *pitayas* were, the 'dragon-fruit' from the cactus. We fell on them, cool and fresh, green and red, the pips giving consistency and asperity to the soft fruit. Then Enrique took us down an old mule track to a lemon grove, where the lemons were big, green and so sweet you could bite into them. No one had ever told me that lemons could be green, or eaten straight. I felt like a wartime evacuee in the countryside seeing a cow for the first time.

Ed started to do a number: he couldn't face the drive back, so they would have to fly him. Enrique tried to get hold of an available pilot on his short-wave, but no one wanted to fly down into the valley that late in the day because the heat affected the air currents.

We started the return journey. Again I rode in the back of the pick-up truck, but the truck was still kicking, so we put in sandbags to weigh it down even more. I felt light-headed with the heat and with the intoxication of the fruit still inside me. I also had a horrible, melancholy feeling that all this couldn't last; that the delightful mindlessness of days lurching around in a pick-up truck under the sun would have to give way to something a little more responsible. I was also worried about the Oldsmobile back in Hidalgo del Parral, which I imagined to be, if not vandalised, at least stripped of its parts or auctioned off at a police benefit ball.

I had a friend in Tahonas, Carlos, an engineer in his twenties who had his own pick-up truck. He had his eye on the daughter of one of the *ejido* bosses. As he knew the father was away in Parral, we drove up and asked to see him, and of course got invited in by the daughter, a well-built, corn-fed girl, who chatted timidly about her graduation prospects. Then the mother came in, a smiling Señora who rambled on about how *celosa*, 'jealous', she was about her daughters, thank God that none of her sons was a drunkard, how she didn't think girls should marry before twenty-seven (as all this came out, various children passed backwards and forwards between the kitchen and the bedrooms, including the daughter), how her son's marriage broke up after two weeks, how even as we spoke the daughter was talking out of the bedroom window with *su novio*, 'her boyfriend' (she gave a sly glance at Carlos, whose face fell), but she only let her do this once a week.

Laughing, I told Carlos afterwards that he was going to have a hard time with the daughter. Carlos launched into a long, over-detailed speech about his sexual frustrations, how primitive the *sierra* was, how he had been trying to make love to a girl in his pick-up and the police had drawn up and he had been forced to get out of the car with his cock hanging out and how – here he turned imploringly to me – how the only Mexican girls he could find who would 'go the distance with him', as he put it, were nurses, and the nearest hospital was many miles away in Parral.

When we went to a local dance I could see the problem for myself. The dance was in Guadalupe y Calvo, a town notorious for its drug-runners and fights. There were drive-in liquor stores where you didn't even have to get out of the car to buy more tequila. Carlos told me how he had been sitting having a meal when a guy at the next table had drawn a gun on someone and killed him. The local drug-runners had developed a nasty way of dealing with any American drug agents they caught: they would bend them over backwards and pour bottles of Coca-Cola down their noses. The Coke would fill up their lungs, eventually drowning the *Yanqui federales*. It seemed a grotesque, metaphoric way to die, like a Jacobean tragedy where someone has to kiss a poisoned skull, or in this case *la bebida imperialista*, 'the imperialist soft drink'.

Yet the dance was a sedate affair – a row of men huddled on one side of the hall, girls on the other and no one dancing, for all the world like a Home Counties village fête. The men muttered into their beers, but didn't dare approach any of the women in case of public rejection.

As an outsider, and after a few beers, I felt less inhibited, and asked a pretty girl in a green dress called Rosario to do me the honour. I was used to the free-form, do-what-you-want-style dancing of a British club: plenty of jumping around to start with and then a grope with the slow number at the end. Unfortunately there were no role models already on the floor to copy for the formal dance that Rosario indicated was now expected. She had asked my name using a formal Spanish that the young never used with each other: '*Cómo se llama Ud?*'

We found ourselves going round in ever decreasing circles as the band played a mournful *corrida* about the death of some bandit in the hills. To make matters worse, Rosario had stopped talking completely and was looking at the floor as we perambulated around with the whole hall watching. Mortified, I joined the men at the back of the hall. Maybe this had happened to all of them once, and as a result they had never danced again.

When Carlos and I drove back along the appalling potholed road, a bunch of drunks screeched by, firing their guns and bouncing their truck into the air. They were clearly letting off a little tension after an evening of never having had the courage to ask a woman to dance. It was *una cosa de hombres*, 'a man's thing'.

One day Enrique woke me early in the morning. When I opened the door, there was a deputation of men behind him, all holding their hats. Enrique felt awkward about whatever it was he had to say. He shuffled from side to side. 'Hugo, your lord is dead.' Enrique had picked up something about Mountbatten's assassination on his short-wave.

That evening we drank long and hard into the night. '¡*Asesinos!*' muttered Enrique, as he refilled my glass with tequila. I told Enrique the truth about what had happened to my car and why I was there. I asked for his advice.

Enrique laughed. He knew the policeman. '*No te preocupas.* Don't worry'. By the time I got back to Parral, everything was *arreglado* and fixed.

The Oldsmobile was still exactly where I had left it, behind the police station. They had even put a tarpaulin over it. Enrique had told me what to say, as well as contacting the policeman direct, so to a certain extent we were just going through the motions. There was a particular phrase that had to be used so that honour was satisfied all round (a phrase not to be found in the *South American Handbook*). I waded straight in with it: '¿*No hay otra manera de arreglar la cosa?* Is there no other way of arranging this matter?'

The policeman studied the papers for one last time as if for some legal loophole and then suggested that a donation to the police widows and orphans fund, in cash, might be an appropriate way of showing my contrition. The bribe was a token one by Mexican standards. I should, of course, have offered it in the first place.

We were both left happy as schoolboys by the arrangement. The policeman even bought me a drink. Then he got serious before I drove off. 'Don't try and do this in the DF,' he said, as all Mexicans describe Mexico City (DF is for *Distrito Federal*, the Federal District). 'They'll eat you alive.'

I celebrated at Hidalgo del Parral's best restaurant, the Villa Mexicana. The steak was the size of the plate and came with a cheese sauce. I felt like a successful gold-digger after a strike, with the money from the sawmill burning a hole in my pocket and my car parked outside. I ordered the best wine they had.

There were photos of Pancho Villa on the wall. This was where he had been gunned down in 1923, in the car his widow Doña Luz had shown me; what she hadn't told me was that Pancho had been visiting one of his mistresses at the time. The ambushers on the outskirts of town had shot nine rounds into him, many of them dumdum bullets. He must have died with the post-coital grin still on his face.

No one knew where Villa was buried. Just like his marriages, he had multiple graves: one here in Parral, but another in Chihuahua, and yet a third in Mexico City.

In some ways his assassination was a compliment. Ostensibly by 1923 the Revolution was long over and Villa had retired to a Chihuahua ranch with his soldiers, three 'wives', a mistress and their eight children (although not his official wife Doña Luz, who'd been sent packing). But when an election came up, Villa hinted that he might run for president – and so scared the incumbent holder, his old nemesis Obregón, who knew that Villa embodied the popular spirit of the Revolution in a way he did not, that Obregón condoned his death.

Villa's final years had been sad ones, brutalised by the ten long years of the Revolution and marginalised by the *políticos* in Mexico City. Yet for many of his countrymen and the wider world he still personified the swaggering Mexican *generalísimo*, who could cry one moment and lead a cavalry charge against machine guns the next. As Marlene Dietrich said admiringly in *Touch of Evil* when she played a Mexican brothel keeper, 'He was some kind of a man.'

I wandered down Parral's main street and bought a pair of boots from the shop I had passed on first arriving. They were caribou, at $40 the most expensive in the shop. I settled on a size five heel as something I could just about master, although even flush with success I realised that if worn back in England, people might suspect me of being an Eagles fan, or worse.

They weren't easy to drive in either. I headed on south. The mountains towards Durango reared up like tombstones ahead of me. I pumped the accelerator as hard as the heels would allow. The towns rolled by.

I kept careful accounts as I went along, in the back of my diary. 'Orson Welles' had been right – gas was cheap in Mexico. A full tank (and the Oldsmobile took a very full tank) cost only $10. For this I had Lázaro Cárdenas to thank – the one truly revolutionary president of the *Partido Revolucionario Institucional* (PRI), the Institutional Revolutionary Party that had effectively ruled the country since Pancho Villa's day and the Mexican Revolution.

Cárdenas had nationalised the country's vast supplies of oil in 1938. Foreign companies from Pearson in Britain to Shell and Hearst united in outrage and boycotted Mexican oil. Only the

Second World War lifted the boycott and saved the country: the Allies were desperate for supplies and didn't want to force the Mexicans into the arms of the Axis powers. Although Pemex, the State oil company, was notoriously corrupt, it had become an article of faith for the PRI to keep petrol prices down.

Cárdenas had also promoted the *ejido* system I had seen in the sawmills, cooperatives of workers who had taken over private land holdings – one of the ideals of the Mexican Revolution that had borne fruit. Unfortunately it had only happened in a sporadic, patchwork way around the country and there were still some areas that were as feudal as Scotland, with large landowners dominating.

My accounts for one typical travelling day show that I spent $10 on petrol, $2 on a six-pack of beer to stop the driving getting boring, 50 cents on a shoe clean to keep my new cowboy boots in pristine fettle, $1 to beggars and $3 on a cheap motel for the night. And 50 cents on gum.

The *South American Handbook* was usually beside me on the seat as I drove. It was full of namby-pamby advice about the 101 things you should bring to keep safe, from antibiotics to the spare bath plug I had told Ed MacDonald about. It listed all the approved restaurants and lodgings that other travellers had 'tested'. It was absolutely not the way I wanted to travel. Because it covered the whole continent, it also weighed a ton. I had already carried it too far. At one point, I thought of just cutting out the Mexico section and getting rid of the rest. But now I was coming to places it didn't even list.

Impetuously I threw the whole thing out of the window. In the rear view mirror I watched as the book broke open on the highway, sending the wafer-thin pages blowing back across the desert scrub. I wanted to be on my own, and I was.

PRAWN COAST

E l Espinazo de Diablo, the so-called 'Devil's Backbone', had sounded melodramatic when Enrique had advised me against it. A twisting, circuitous road from Durango over the mountains to the sea, it reminded me of the old Road Runner cartoons, with Wile E. Coyote watching in despair as the Road Runner effortlessly tore up the hairpins ahead of him. It even had those little tunnels around the cliff corners.

When, for the first time in my travels, I saw a Mexican sign warning about danger I began to take the road more seriously. For the first hour or so I accelerated into the curves and braked on the straights, as I remembered an uncle telling me to do. Then I started to relax, and maybe had one beer too many. Either that or I was singing along to the radio too much. Coming a little too fast out of a curve, I managed to hit the accelerator instead of the brake.

It was all over very quickly. The Oldsmobile mounted the road, hit both bollards on the kerb, bounced back the other side of the road and went into the ditch. I clambered out and retched.

A truck had been patiently following me for a while, at a discreet distance. I had occasionally seen it in my mirror. The driver and his mate must have witnessed the whole thing. As the truck went by, they gave me a wide-eyed, wondering look. I was too shocked to ask them to stop.

I crossed back over to the bollards I had knocked down. There was a sheer drop. It was sobering. It had also started to rain.

Not many cars had passed me and none came now. Finally an American Winnebago, of all things, hove into view. Few Americans went down to Mexico on holiday, given that it was on their doorstep, and those that did tended to stick to tried and tested resorts like Acapulco or Cancún.

I had struck lucky. The guy driving, Joe, was in his thirties, bearded and looked like an old counter-culture type who had now started to make money. I assessed the damage with him. The Oldsmobile had got off lightly – it had done more damage to the bollards. A tyre had been slashed on a rock I'd hit and we changed it. The jack Orson had so generously thrown in for free with the car looked like it would need a month's immersion in penetrating oil; we used Joe's gleaming hydraulic one instead.

'Never trust a hippy' had been a tenet of the punk movement, but Joe came good, even if he was playing Quicksilver Messenger Service as he brewed me a restorative mug of coffee. I liked him at once, not least because he was concerned that I was too young to be making this journey – and after the accident I was beginning to get concerned myself. And unlike many of my generation, for whom America was a Darth Vader empire of Smurfs, Disney and serial FM music, I loved almost everything about the country: the space, the optimism and above all the cars; I just wished Americans would start listening to better music again.

'You might need this.' Joe gave me a well-thumbed copy of *The People's Guide to Mexico* by Carl Franz, with a Haight-Ashbury logo and a classic hippy slogan on the front: 'Wherever you go . . . there you are!!', a compendium of advice gleaned from the author's years in Mexico. It covered everything from what to do if you ran over a cactus to obscene Mexican hand-signals, and made no mention of bringing a spare bath plug. I was touched that Joe was just giving it away.

'I'd roll you a joint for the road, man, but it might not help your driving,' said Joe laconically. He must have seen my crestfallen face and opened up a side panel of the Winnebago. Beside the packets of herbal tea and ginseng were five neatly wrapped cellophane bags of what he described as 'pure Sinaloa shit', which he had collected from a farmer near El Fuerte.

'Are you a dealer?' I blurted out, feeling naïve.

Joe laughed: 'Man, when I get back to Portland, my friends and I will get through that in a month – maybe less if we start making hash cookies.'

I liked him so much I thought I'd play him a little of The Clash to see if I could move him on from the Grateful Dead and all those psychedelic workouts. But after listening politely to 'London's Burning', all Joe could say was, 'Maybe you had to have been there.' Which I guess was true.

The Oldsmobile limped on down the road. Although everything seemed to be working, the wheel was scraping badly against the axle with a noise like chalk on a blackboard. It was a relief to reach Mazatlán, the first big port on the Pacific and my first sight of the ocean. There was a picturesque sunset that a Victorian traveller would have swooned at – yellows, reds and 'ochre' I supposed, although I wasn't quite sure what ochre was. To me it looked sickly, like one of those tequila sunsets where the grenadine had coagulated with the orange juice into a glutinous mess that seemed a waste of good tequila.

Behind the big formal boulevard along the seafront was an underdeveloped strip of sand and rock called Olas Altas, where the big breakers came in. I double-parked, tore off my filthy clothes and boots and sprinted for the sea in Marks & Spencer Y-fronts. A smart Mexican family who were promenading up and down the boulevard for their evening *paseo* did a double take. I must have looked a strange sight, with a deep farmer's tan on my neck and arms from the mountains, and lily-white skin everywhere else.

After months in the mountains, I was desperate to get into the Pacific. It was too rocky to swim much, so I stood in the impact zone of the breakers and let the waves hammer down on me.

Afterwards I ate a dish that had five types of prawn in it. I was used to only one type – cocktail – so diffidently asked the waiter what they were. It was his cue. The restaurant was half-empty, as it was off-season, so he could hold forth at length about the prawn, its habits and history. He was a lugubrious man with the studied sadness of the professional waiter, but this was a subject that animated him.

'Did you know,' he said, 'that the prawn, alone of all creatures and indeed of all *humanidad* as well,' he paused to let me reflect on the enormity of this, 'that the prawn is the only thing that has had two entire countries named after it?' I didn't. Nor could I think of them.

'Cameroon and Gambia,' he proclaimed proudly (from *camarón* and *gamba*, different Spanish terms for prawn). I ate mine with renewed respect. He reappeared with a steaming plate of red snapper in a garlic sauce, which I hadn't ordered. 'On the house,' he said. 'I like a man who likes his prawns.'

Mazatlán was too big for me. Although it had some fine beaches stretching away to the north, it was an industrial port. I watched the dockers loading up Chinese boats with cotton, *chicle* (chewing gum) and more of the famous prawns. The trade route over to China in the west had always been important to Mexico ever since an enterprising monk, Andrés de Urdaneta, had proved the Pacific passage was possible by sailing east from the Philippines to Mexico in 1565, the mirror image of Columbus's original journey from Spain. Although no one ever remembers Urdaneta, his journey was as important to Spain as Columbus's, for it enabled luxury goods like silk and spices to come over the Pacific in the 'China ships'; they would be exchanged at ports like Mazatlán and Acapulco for local produce, and brought by mule over the highlands to Veracruz on the Gulf of Mexico, before being shipped to Spain.

As long as no British privateer caught the boats in transit, this was a lucrative trade that kept Mexico rich long after the Aztec coffers had been plundered and exhausted. As a result Mexico was awash with *chinoiserie* and many of the costumes people think of as being more Mexican than a tortilla would never have evolved without the Chinese influence.

*

I wanted something a little funkier than Mazatlán, more like the old resort Richard Burton had gone to in *The Night of the Iguana*. I found it further down the coast, at San Blas.

San Blas (pronounced 'blah') had once been a flourishing port like Mazatlán, with some 30,000 people. Now the ruins of the custom house and Spanish fortress had been left some way behind the shoreline and the sand had come in to fill what had been the original bay. The sand was still coming. In the only place to stay, the Hotel Bucanero, the taciturn owner spent most of his time brushing it out of his weed-blown yard.

When I said I'd stay for a while, he let me have the only high room there was, with a balcony that looked over the village. There was a broken-down rocking chair that came with the room, and I could sit out on it, drinking Pacífico beer and watching the pelicans flying over towards the sea. The white tower and walls of an unfinished church protruded through the palms below like the bleached spine and ribcage of some stranded whale.

The first evening I went down to the beach. There were the dying embers of a fire where the local boys had been cooking fish, but no one was around. When I got out of the car, I realised why.

Years later I met Iggy Pop, one of my idols, when I was doing some film work. He had a face that looked like it had been to many different planets, seen the death of several suns and lived to tell the tale. Iggy was unexpectedly loquacious and in the course of talking around the houses, it turned out he had bummed around Mexico himself at one point. He too had been to San Blas – perhaps where his 'Blah! Blah! Blah!' song had come from. His face lit up: 'Yeah, San Blas! Those fucking midges!'

They ate me alive. In seconds, they had got inside my clothes, my ear, seemingly every crevice of my body. I got back to the hotel and rinsed myself in tequila and mouthwash, the only liquids I had to hand (the shower didn't work). From then on I stuck to watching the sunsets from the balcony.

There weren't many other people staying in the hotel, but I got to know a young Brazilian couple. He was bearded, while she was pretty in a quiet, melancholy way. They were travelling up through South America as an extended honeymoon and had already been gone a year. 'We are tired of it,' said Clara, in her Spanish with its curious rolling Portuguese accent. Clara was tired of most things.

The only place she had really liked on their travels had been the Galapagos Islands, 'because you can touch the animals'.

The military government in Brazil forced travellers to leave a large bond if they went abroad, as security that they would return. This seemed curious to me. Wouldn't anyone in their right minds want to go back to Brazil? It was always portrayed as a bounty-bar paradise of earthly riches. Hadn't Ronnie Biggs (a hero of the Sex Pistols) made it his ultimate destination?

I used to see Clara and Juan on the beach, taking childish pleasure in building sandcastles together. They were both slim and tanned – a golden boy and girl – but there was a curious sad ennui that seemed to hang over them. I noticed it particularly in Clara's eyes.

My bedroom was directly above theirs and during siestas and at night I would hear them making love through the thin floor and try not to think about it too much. This was difficult, as Juan would keep shouting out numbers in Portuguese in the middle of it all. What were they? Code-numbers for particular sexual positions he wanted to adopt, like an American football coach calling out the moves? Or an indication of what stage of arousal he'd reached, like Dinah Washington in that wonderful song 'TV is the Thing' when the TV repairman turns her dial all the way up to eleven. I tried not to speculate, but it was enough to keep me awake and sweating.

The best and just about only place to eat in town was called Diligencias, run by a fat Indian woman who would swat with casual ferocity at flies as she took orders. The flies were too slow for her and the walls were covered in their corpses. The house speciality was turtle steak, even though they were a protected species. For breakfast, she handed out plates of *huevos rancheros*, so-called 'ranch eggs' with a tomato and chili sauce, not that I had ever seen them during my time in the actual ranches of the desert and hills; the orange juice had raw egg stirred into it, 'for the blood sugar' she claimed, although the salmonella count was probably high as well.

This was where the surfers hung out. San Blas was famous for having a long breaking wave that curled right across the bay. If I hadn't known this before, I soon felt familiar with its every last idiosyncrasy; the American surf-bums held forth at length over their turtle steaks about the wave's remarkable properties.

I would give them lifts down to the beach in the Oldsmobile in the morning, and made a point of playing them my Beach Boys tape. Once I got to know them better, they told me that they all hated the Beach Boys; to a man they preferred my punk music as it was more aggressive, and surfing is a sport rippling with aggression.

They taught me how to surf after a fashion. I borrowed an old-style 'woodie', a board almost 12 feet long, unlike the usual short ones designed to emulate the quick manoeuvrability of skateboards. This board was so big you could invite a friend on and have lunch with him – or for that matter fit an outboard motor. If I ever got up and running with a wave, I wasn't able to do any fancy manoeuvres, but at least I was unlikely to fall off.

What impressed me was the incredible speed with which the wave took you: the beach seemed to track in towards me as I stayed still on the board, like a trick camera shot.

Not that I got up on the board that often. We did what it has to be said a lot of surfers spend most of their time doing – staying out behind the breakers, lying on our boards, chewing the fat and occasionally, but only occasionally, making a half-hearted attempt to catch a wave. We would justify this on the grounds that a better set would soon be coming in, or that the wave was breaking further down. Unlike skiing, where there is no real excuse for waiting at the top of the mountain, with surfing you can always find a reason why a particular wave doesn't have your number on it. And still walk up onto the beach holding your board and feeling like a hero.

There was a collection of shacks on the beach made up of interleaved palms that the local boys had laboriously assembled. I say 'boys' not patronisingly, but because their average age was about fifteen. With true Mexican ingenuity, they had expanded from the original bar where they served up their fish by building on annexes in a beach-bum parody of a luxury hotel. There was, for instance, a small section where we could sling hammocks to sleep off the siesta. When after a few weeks I complained that my car was getting too hot by the end of each day (we would head back late afternoon, before the midges came out), they built on an extra section for it, which we dubbed the 'carport'.

After surfing, we would eat the fish that the boys cooked on fires, sleep off a siesta and then douse ourselves in pure coconut oil so that we fried up in the sun playing football.

There were a lot of drifters about the place. San Blas seemed to accumulate them, like the sand: people who had come for days and stayed for months, probably because it was dirt-cheap, easy-going and the police were noticeable for their low profile. Some travellers stayed in town, some in an old moth-eaten trailer park out by the dunes.

The surfer I talked to most was called Alex. He was remarkable for having only one leg; he had lost the other in Vietnam. He would drag himself up onto his knee and come in on the board that way.

It wasn't really so much a case of talking to Alex as Alex talking at me. He took me laboriously through his whole Vietnam campaign. I was bored shitless by this – it was, after all, a hippy war. All this stuff about 'gooks'. The more I told him I wasn't interested, the more Alex talked about it, as if he thought I was putting him down.

But Alex had some other, funnier stories. He was down in Mexico because he could get some 'serious codeine supplies' without prescription – not for pain relief, but because he enjoyed the high. He wasn't eligible for an army pension for some obscure reason, so was getting his welfare cheques sent down to Mexico. I imagined trying to sell that one to the Department of Health and Social Security back in Britain.

He had a fabulously filthy mind. When lying on the beach after lunch, Alex would watch one of the beautiful American surfer girls as she walked down to the water and invent a whole pageant of erotic rites for her. Coconut oil would always come into it at some point in the proceedings, usually as a finale. 'And then I'd take the coconut oil and I'd . . .' With some obscene gesture, he would shiver all over and rub more oil over his chest.

I drove up with him to a deserted beach he knew some miles up the coast. Alex said he didn't fancy a swim himself so I went in on my own. I loved to swim anyway, so spent a while floating up and down with the current. When I came back up, he was lying against a palm with his artificial leg off and smiling a strange smile.

'How come no one swims here, Alex?'

'Because you know what they call this beach? Shark beach.'

'Very funny.'

Alex held up the noticeboard he had carefully concealed: '*Peligro! Tiburones!* Danger! Sharks!'

'You fucking bastard.'

'Hey, you survived. Anyway, if you'd lost a leg or an arm, you'd be like me.' It was hard to tell if it was a joke or a test.

That night we got drunk together in a little cantina down a backstreet. A *cantina* is a qualitatively different experience in Mexico from a bar. A bar is a place to have a social drink, maybe a serious social drink, but no more. A *cantina* is a place they carry you out feet first. This was a typical sawdust *cantina*, with a flimsy curtain screening it from the street, some bare tables and a hard-looking woman presiding over proceedings.

The radio was playing 'Mi Guajirita', the great lament of the Mexican male whose 'Guajirita' loved him totally and would kill him if his own love wavered, yet he still demanded that she love him even more. The chorus swelled up into the repeated and desperate '*Quiéreme, quiéreme más / quiéreme, quiéreme más*, love me, love me more / love me, love me more.'

Alex had stopped talking much. We were concentrating on getting drunk, not always as easy with tequila as you might think. Alex had given me his theory on this before – that it was like surfing, you could drink for a while and it wouldn't take you but suddenly you'd take a hit and get carried full force towards the shore. For the while, we were still paddling around with neat tequilas and the odd Pacífico beer as a chaser.

The radio was playing more laments: the *negrita* who left her man; the need to go East, '*al Oriente*', not to China in this case, but to the east of Cuba where a lot of the original salsa songs came from.

It was Alex who had the hit of tequila that first pulled the trigger. He began to weave in time to the music. 'Man, I didn't really fight in Vietnam at all. I went there as a hospital auxiliary. I mean, let me tell you, that was fighting as well. I lost the leg in a road accident a few years ago.'

I was beyond caring. By the time I put the glass down, the

biggest wave that I had ever felt in my life had picked me up like a rag doll and was hurtling me at speed towards the rocks.

I made it back to the hotel, although I'm not sure how. Sometime in the middle of the night I went into the bathroom to vomit, steering by the noise of the plumbing and turned on the light to see the biggest cockroach in the world sitting on my toothbrush. I vowed I would never drink again.

The fat woman in Diligencias was sympathetic the next morning. She gave me an extra egg in my orange juice to help with what she thought was a bad case of low blood sugar. I finally understood the term the surfers had used to describe being wiped out and chewed up by a particularly fearsome wave: 'an ice-cream head'.

The surfers were already down at the beach. I followed and tried to park in my usual place under the palm shacks. Nothing was coordinating. I missed badly and knocked out one of the palm supports holding the 'carport' up. In a slow-motion blur, I watched the boys' adjoining palm shacks all collapse in a sort of awful domino effect.

The boys looked at me. They didn't say anything, but it was time to leave San Blas.

*

As I drove on south I found myself for the first time beginning to resent the car. Every time that I found a place I really liked – the cattle ranch, the mountains, San Blas – it forced me to move on. Far from being the agent of liberation I had hoped it would be – 'young man has car, will travel' – it brought police attention, hassles and above all responsibilities, with the continual worry of whether I would ever get it down to Central America in one piece. This was perhaps a one-sided way of putting the argument, but that's what happens in relationships. And that's what it had become – a relationship.

I had deliberately chosen not to have a human companion for the trip, figuring that sooner or later we would start arguing and that I would always be bumping into other people for company. Instead I now found myself bound inextricably to a hunk of machinery. It was no longer just a fun thing; we were married, with thousands of miles to go.

Nor was the Oldsmobile looking its best. Already the mountains and the bad roads had taken their toll, as had all the things I kept hitting. A hub cap had fallen off. Grains of sand had got stuck in the electric windows and they were making a grating sound.

The last straw came as I was driving along a small lane by the shores of Lake Chapala, a large inland lake set in the mountains. Now that I was getting closer to the more populated areas of Central Mexico and the highlands, I had been trying where possible to take smaller roads to avoid police roadblocks.

Because I was taking in the view, I was driving more slowly than usual. There were beautiful pink ferns that caught the sunset and glowed softly. The car suddenly dropped dead in the road.

Literally dropped. There was a cut-out circular hole in the road into which one of the wheels had rolled as neatly as a golfball. Lying by the side of the road, as if in a practical joke, was the manhole cover.

I got out of the car. 'Fuck, fuck and fuck again.' I couldn't believe it. I could have cried. I certainly didn't know what I was going to do. The wheel was completely wedged down the hatch, with the whole car tilted onto its axle, like a man with his hand down a hole.

It was getting dark. I thought of walking to the nearest town and throwing myself on someone's mercy to get hold of a fork-lift truck. Nothing else would get me out.

An Indian man came by on a bicycle and stopped to see what had happened. He looked a bit like Norman Wisdom.

'What you need,' he said, 'is a pole.'

I was in no mood for stupidities. 'There are no poles,' I said flatly.

He took out his machete, went over to a sapling growing by the water's edge and cut it down with some vigorous hacks.

'There.'

Two guys came by on a motorbike. They helped roll a boulder beside the wheel and we used it to try to lever the wheel up, the four of us hanging off the pole like that picture of the Marines desperately trying to raise the American flag on Iwo Jima. It was hopeless. The wheel lifted about an inch and then plopped back into its hole.

A truck came by carrying high explosives. By now I was getting tired of explaining what had happened. I felt like just asking the driver for some explosives and putting the car out of its misery.

At the back of his truck, the driver had a hoist. He lifted the car up while we levered the other side. It worked. The wheel popped out like a cork.

Remarkably, there wasn't a scratch on the Oldsmobile. I had some beers in the boot and distributed them round. Then we wheeled the manhole cover over and discovered why it had been left to one side. It was the wrong size. So I left the pole sticking out of the hole as a warning to any other motorists who might come after me.

That night I slept out by the lakeside on an old tarpaulin one of the surfers had given me. It was a clear night and I could see the stars. I felt good again about the car, as if we'd had an argument that had cleared the air. I also realised that I was beginning to fall in love with Mexico itself. This had snuck up on me slowly and a little to my surprise. There was something so appealing about the cards the country kept dealing me: so moral when you needed help, so amoral when you wanted wildness. I began to realise too that I didn't understand it at all.

There were horses grazing on the lake shore and I woke several times during the night to find them moving around me. I had an odd, hallucinatory thought as I lay there in half-sleep, hearing the movements of the horses, that the stars above me were light coming through pinpricks in a tent above.

At dawn I watched a lone fisherman move along the lake casting a small, weighted, round net into the shallows with assured, casual Mexican skill. Any big fish he kept, but the small ones he threw onto the rocks with equally casual Mexican cruelty. As he worked his way along, I followed, throwing the little fish back in.

I ate a breakfast of bananas and grapes further down the lake at Ajijic, watching the washerwomen laughing in their wet nylon blouses and heavy dresses. Later still, I stopped to watch a wedding procession stream out of the beautiful church in Jacotopec, confetti settling on the mariachi suits of the musicians as they played the bride and groom out.

This was D. H. Lawrence country. He came here towards the end of his 'savage pilgrimage' in search of the elemental and non-Western. The states of Jalisco and Michoacán around the lake were, for him, the Mexican heartland – a strong Indian presence and a place of pre-Columbian history, without the intervening modern complications that Mexico City threw up. Most of *The Plumed Serpent* was written while he stayed on the lake.

I read it over the next couple of days and found it a remarkably flawed book. Lawrence had grafted his demons and ghosts onto the Mexico he wanted to find. The two Mexican male protagonists become not only revolutionary leaders, but resurrected incarnations of the Aztec deities Quetzalcoatl and Huitzilopochtli, who among other things, revive the ancient (and it is implied, noble) tradition of human sacrifice.

All this is witnessed by Kate, the Western observer who mediates the story and drifts through the book alternately attracted and repelled by the willpower of the men. There follows a certain amount of the usual Lawrence guff about sex: 'She swooned prone beneath ... the ancient phallic mystery, the ancient god-devil of the male Pan'; and some excellent descriptive passages where Lawrence confines himself to simple observation of life around the lake. But what annoyed me was the novel's core obsession with reviving the pre-Columbian way of life. The sequences describing human sacrifice, with their chanting and theatrics, were like a bad Ken Russell movie. This, Lawrence seemed to say, was the true Mexico, which Mexico now needed to find again. Anything since the Spanish conquest was a false consciousness that should be scraped away.

It was an idea that I had come across before. I had seen the great murals of Orozco, the revolutionary painter, where Cortés was portrayed putting Montezuma to heel, the noble savage helpless before the conquistador's greed. It was a staple tenet of the Revolution that they were restoring the land 'to the Indians'. Half the towns in Mexico had statues to Cuauhtémoc, the last Aztec emperor, while Cortés reputedly only had one in the entire country.

I was suspicious. It all seemed a little too easy. From their base at Tenochtitlán, now Mexico City, the Aztecs had maintained a vicious system of tribute over other subjected nations – like the Tarascans who would presumably have been living around this lake. The tribute was not only in slaves and goods, but in fodder for their increasingly large festivals of human sacrifice.

The actual reign of the Aztecs was relatively short. They dominated the centre of Mexico properly for only some two hundred years before Cortés's arrival. Driven by a greed equal to anything the Spaniards were to reveal later, they had mercilessly conquered neighbouring tribes under the direction of emperors who worked closely with priests (indeed some emperors, like Montezuma, had previously been head priests).

As the priests assumed more and more control of the Aztec war machine, so the human sacrifices had grown to a startling extent. By the time the Spaniards arrived, they were killing 20,000 captives a year, ripping out their hearts on the tops of pyramids in mass ceremonies and letting the blood run down charnel channels cut into the stairways.

What had started as a way of propitiating the gods had become a useful way of reminding tribute tribes who was in charge. In a chillingly Orwellian way, artificial wars were created, the so-called 'wars of flowers', in which the Aztecs would force tribes they had already conquered to meet them in combat again in order to furnish their war gods with sacrificial victims properly taken in battle. It was hard to excuse this brutality on the grounds of 'different value systems' – not unless you could exonerate Pol Pot on the same grounds. The human sacrifices were only the most extreme representation of a culture that was driven by religious guilt and bloodlust to an extent that must have made the Catholicism of the Spanish Inquisition seem mild, if recognisable, by comparison.

My sense of Mexico was that the Spanish invasion had brought an unexpected fusion of two very different cultures. The two races discovered, after the initial shock of confrontation, that they had a great deal in common. Among other things, there seemed to have been considerable sexual attraction. Spaniards and natives interbred at considerable speed and even in Mexico now, while there might be financial discrimination against the Indians, there was little racial prejudice (if anything there were more insults hurled at people with fair, European skins – like me).

The conquerors had their faults, and of course wreaked considerable destruction, let alone bringing smallpox and other Old World diseases, but their influence had not been as malign as Lawrence and others implied. The strengths of the Aztecs – or more properly the Náhuatl or Mexica, as the archaeologists called them – their dexterity, their phenomenal sculptural and craft skills, even the name of the country, had all been preserved. The Spanish colonial style, with its churches, its big central squares, the *'zócalos'* of every town, was a considerable addition. And nobody could tell me that the human sacrifices could be condoned on the liberal cop-out of 'cultural difference'.

After all, I reflected as I cruised around in the Oldsmobile, without Cortés the Mexicans would never have had wheels.

A surfer back in San Blas had played me a Neil Young song, 'Cortez The Killer', which showed that the same romantic Lawrentian myth was still around: in Young's version of the Conquest, when Cortés came 'dancing across the water, with his galleons and guns,' he was met by a New Age Montezuma who gathered his subjects around him with coca leaves and pearls; the women were all beautiful, the men stood straight and strong, 'Hate was just a legend and war was never known'. This was the paradise that the brutal 'Cortez, Cortez, what a killer' supposedly destroyed.

Remembering this only strengthened my feeling that it was a hippy con. 'Hate was just a legend' indeed. And didn't Neil Young wear long suede jackets, with fringed braids? He was one of the reasons punk had happened. Along with Pancho Villa, Cortés belonged right up there in my pantheon of Mexican heroes.

The 'real' Mexico was not some archaeological secret to be uncovered and revived – it was in my face and now.

Of the many British writers who had flocked to Mexico in the 1930s, the one who echoed this best was Evelyn Waugh, ever the iconoclast. He disagreed completely with the Lawrentian view: 'his loneliness and lack of humour and his restless neurotic imagination combine to make [*The Plumed Serpent*] one of the silliest stories in recent literature'.

Instead, Waugh proposed, 'The traditions of Spain are still deep in the Mexican character and I believe that it is only by developing them that the country can ever grow happy.' He went on to note, astutely, that 'Mexicans feel like Aztecs but think like Spaniards'.

His book *Robbery Under Law: The Mexican Object-Lesson* has been ignored by many readers, not least because Waugh himself chose to ignore it, excluding it from a later anthology of his travel writing and describing it as 'like an interminable *Times* leader of 1880'. Its cumbersome title and provenance are off-putting; Waugh only wrote the book because he was commissioned to do so by the Pearson family, whose British oilfields had been expropriated by the Mexicans.

But it contains some of his best travel writing. Like Graham Greene, he arrived in Mexico in 1939 when the country was in tumult and mirrored some of the political divisions that were emerging in Europe. Waugh was too good an author to stick to the Pearson brief and something of the casual cruelty and honesty of Mexico both appealed and appalled:

The fascination of Mexico lies in the stimulus it gives to the imagination. Anything may happen there; almost everything has happened there; it has seen every extreme of human nature, good, bad and ridiculous. It has, in a way, the position toward Europe that Africa had to the Romans: a source of novelty.

*

The main town in the area was Chapala, which had a calm Sunday-morning feel: kids playing marbles on the sidewalk, mariachi musicians propositioning passers-by, families taking a *paseo* up and down the boulevards. The quiet small-town feeling was restful. It was good to see people gossiping, reading papers, falling asleep under the trees in the *zócalo*. As a traveller, I was beginning to crave such quotidian, domestic normality.

I sat in the park facing the lake. There were piers with candy-striped awnings and little launches taking day-trippers out onto the water.

Watching the young couples holding hands, I tried to remember the last time I had seen teenagers doing the same back home. A curious thing had happened before I left England: overnight, every girl started to wear black, as if by religious proclamation. They cruised down the high streets of the country on a Saturday after-noon, Boots eyeliner, leather jackets and spiked hair to the fore, perhaps, for the more daring, with a token zip or chain. Pale skinny boys might sometimes be in attendance, if they were not under-age drinking in some pub that looked the other way. A friendly punch was about as near as the two sexes came to any public display of physical affection.

Seeing these young couples, '*novios*', that delicate Spanish word meaning both 'lovers' and 'fiancés', made me feel world-weary by comparison. They looked like they were still listening to David Cassidy records as they sat decorously on the benches together.

The boys bought red roses from the vendors or paid a crazed, elderly photographer to take their joint portraits with an old-fashioned camera that had a hood coming out of the back (surely for effect?).

A shoe-shine boy made a pitch to clean my caribou cowboy boots. I sized him up, unsure if he was man enough for the job. He had wide, wondering eyes. I told him that I came from England, which was directly the other side of the Earth if you burrowed a hole directly under where we were sitting. This blew his mind: '¡*Híjole!*' He must have been about twelve. When I told him that it rained there a lot, he persuaded me to add special water-protective lacquer to the boots as all-weather protection.

The kids were an entrepreneurial bunch. After the shoe-shine boy, I was offered an array of plastic boats and stringy little hammocks. 'What you really should be selling', I told them, 'are single cigarettes.' This was an idea I had long held – that for those too mean, impecunious or liable to chain-smoke if left with an entire pack, like myself, what you needed were a supply of single cigarettes constantly to hand. They grasped the principle immediately: 'So if we bought a packet of twenty for 10 pesos, we could sell each one for a peso.'

They asked me if I painted my lips. This wasn't meant as a taunt; I had noticed before that Mexicans who didn't come across many Europeans or Americans were surprised how red our lips were compared to their own more brown ones.

The mariachis were doing a brisk business in the sun. Their tunics were glittering; they had more braid and silver on them than admirals of the fleet, with red cummerbands over impressive paunches. I admired one trumpet player who always had a cigarette on the go, tucked still lit behind the keys during the breaks between brass sections.

Tired of reading D. H. Lawrence, I picked up some old Mexican comics that were lying on the bench. Their unlikely heroine was called Hermelinda, a grotesque, ulcer-ridden hag with a sharp sense of humour and a penchant for necrophilia. She led her gang of kids in cheerful exploits that often ended in a bit of grave-robbing and a quick hug with a corpse. I didn't need Lawrence to tell me that this was a country that had, to say the least, an unusual attitude towards death.

A wan youth approached and asked, lisping, if I liked reading and what *The Plumed Serpent* was about. When I told him that it was set in Mexico, he asked that I translate a page or two of it, which I did with embarrassment. A small group of vendors stopped to listen. Translating 'she was not herself, she was gone, and her own desires were gone in the ocean of the great desire. As the man whose fingers touched her was gone in the ocean that is male, stooping over the face of the waters' demanded linguistic acrobatics as well as considerable nerve.

My audience loved it. The more sonorous, euphonic and just plain daft that Lawrence got, the more the swirling, rhetorical cadences of Spanish made it sound as if I were delivering the goods. That most of it made no sense at all seemed to heighten my audience's enjoyment.

I was reprieved when the wan youth announced he would like to read his own poetry. The audience melted away. I soon realised why. The poetry was of a cloying, greeting-card sentimentality that was too much for even the Mexicans' saccharine taste. Roses melted to desire at every verse. Whenever I told him I had heard enough, he would beg me to listen to another until I resorted to point-blank insults: 'These poems are terrible. Leave me alone. I want to read *Hermelinda*.' He sensed he was dealing with a lost soul and moved on to harass other victims.

I was running out of the money I had earned at the sawmill. That night, still in the park, I prepared to doss down on one of the benches and ate cheaply from the nearby stalls: corn on the cob, with a smear of red chilli sauce on it, and lemons stuffed with coconut. A vendor was selling black-market shrimps; during the proscribed breeding season, those who couldn't live without them were prepared to pay the hefty extra premium. I remembered the waiter with his global prawn-power theories. Crustaceans were clearly the market to be in.

The park's population changed with the dark. The families left and roving bands of lads started to lurch around. Some of them offered me rum and Coke, a drink strictly for the girls back in England; but this was not the time to get precious with a group who were on the borderline between conviviality and abuse. One of them, a butcher, told me: 'We are the fucked-up sons, *los hijos de putamadre*, of the Virgin of Guadalupe and Uncle Sam.' I nodded politely. He pointed a wavering finger at the plastic bottle of Coke, which they were mixing into the rum with dangerous imprecision. '*Ron y coca*, rum and Coke, that's what we are, rum and Coke.'

We sat up late, putting the world to rights on the park bench. They could recite the names of the entire England football squad, which was more than I could. When they left, I wanted to sleep out on the park bench, but the thought of any wandering and less amiable youths practising their *Clockwork Orange* techniques on me, or any little tricks they'd learnt from *Hermelinda*, was unnerving; I slept in the car. I felt safe there.

To Mexico City

He was a boy of about twelve, in thin clothes and bare feet, standing shivering by the side of the road. I stopped to give him a lift and turned the Oldsmobile's powerful heater on full.

I had reached the hills south of Chapala, as I wove my way circuitously over to Mexico City by the back roads. The mists had come down, delicately fringing the hillsides and it had started to rain.

I made a point of always picking up hitch-hikers. The Oldsmobile had already carried old women clutching turkeys (I was worried they would shit on the upholstery), two beautiful American girls called, satisfyingly, Cindy and Nancy, and a stranded truck driver who looked like a Mexican Marlon Brando and never said a word, even when I played him Sex Pistols tapes.

The Indian kid was called Eloi. He came from the next village up ahead, Angahuan. I asked him what he knew of the nearby volcano of Paricutín, which I was curious about.

The boy took a big breath: 'A man came into our village one day and said that his land had started to grow hot, and smoke had started to come out and he had put his hat over the smoke but it hadn't done any good and the ground had opened up like a field of trumpets. And the trumpets had just kept on growing, with great *tremores* racking the countryside, and volcanic dust covering the good green land, and the lava flowing over a whole village, which is called San Juan, so that only the church steeples can still be seen. And the villagers, as we were simple Tarascans, were afraid until a gringo professor came and told us what it was, a volcano. And now the people have no money, because the dust has covered our fields.'

I drove Eloi up a gravelled track filled with potholes to the village. His mother gave me coffee and with the overpowering and generous hospitality of all Mexicans, particularly poor ones, pressed tacos stuffed with sweet potato on me, with *atole*, a drink like a sweet, thin porridge. '*Mi casa es su casa*, my house is your house,' she said, using the familiar mantra.

She talked to her daughters and Eloi in the Tarascan dialect. She told me that this was one of the last villages where it was still spoken, but in the village school the children were forced to speak *castellano* – literally 'Castilian' Spanish, as the Mexicans always described it rather than *mejicano*, their own dialects.

Angahuan was a desperately poor village, with the only bare-footed Mexicans I had seen on my travels; pigs lay in the alleys between the damp, thatched cottages. The women wore sombre blue-and-black-striped cloaks. I saw some in a shop and felt them – they were cheap and thin, machine-made. Any cloaks they wove themselves, the woman in the shop told me, were sold for food, as they fetched a far higher price.

Eloi must have learnt his description of Paricutín's eruption by

74

rote, as it had happened some years before his birth, in 1947. He took me to the remains of the neighbouring village of San Juan, which the lava had covered completely. We walked a mile or so through the drizzle and the mist to get there.

There was an awful desolation of lava as we approached. The only sign that the village had existed at all was the top of a church spire poking out. The actual volcano, which had risen up out of nothing to a height of 8,000 feet, was some way distant and hidden by the clouds. San Juan had only just been covered by the very edge of the lava flow.

There was an incongruity about the church spires set in a jumble of volcanic rock, like some Buñuel creation; he would have loved to submerge the whole Catholic Church in red hot lava. It was a haunting image to carry with me as I drove on through the twisting mountains.

I was beginning to feel odd, half-nauseous and delirious. I stopped for water and a rest, then carried on. As soon as I got in the car and started again it got worse. I stopped again and looked under the car. The exhaust pipe had fallen off (either weakened by my plunge down the manhole or on one of the interminable small potholes I kept hitting) and carbon monoxide had been pouring into the car. I was surprised I hadn't heard the exhaust fall off, but I usually had the music on loud.

A mechanic in the next town didn't have the right exhaust. He recommended waiting until I got to Mexico City. Instead we lashed up some oil cans jammed together over the exhaust as a temporary measure. Driving on I couldn't tell if it was working; I felt as if I was being dosed with a mixture of amyl nitrate and cider.

So when I finally came into Mexico City at dusk, it was like entering hell. The traffic snarled with ferocity: although I'd come in on a small road, it quickly funnelled into a larger road, then a larger one again with six or seven 'lanes': 'lanes' because, if anything, the dividing marks were seen as provocation by the red-blooded local drivers, who straddled them, cut across them or ignored them, but made sure never to follow them. When we did stop for traffic lights, a flood of vendors and aggressive touting screen-wipers would surge over the cars before being swept away on the green.

It was *Death Race 2000*: there were neon signs flashing, my head felt like it was coming apart, there were seemingly no street directions and no way of knowing where I was – I had no city road map. I ended up on the *Periférico*, the Ring Road, circling round and round like the damned in Dante's *Inferno*; at last I saw a familiar name and somehow got off to where I wanted to go.

I remembered Jack Kerouac and Neal Cassady arriving here *On The Road*, 'all of Mexico City stretched out on its volcanic crater below and spewing city smokes and early dusklights'. Mexico had been their promised land, the rainbow at the end of the beatniks' thousand-mile rampaging through the more ordered world of 1950s' America, where the scroll of Kerouac's stream-of-consciousness writing finally ran out (according to some accounts because the dog ate the end of the single long sheet of paper he had used to write *On The Road*): 'We had finally found the magic land at the end of the road and we never dreamed the extent of the magic either.'

I had been in Mexico City before, of course, when I had first arrived and earned the money to buy the car. It was a fabulous city, a city of fables and secrets, from the Aztec pyramids that were only now being excavated under the main square to the teeming life of the suburbs and slums. It was also a place that ran on faster time than the rest of the country. The biggest city in the world when Cortés entered it in 1519, and still the biggest now.

In my time away, and lulled by the thousands of miles of empty Mexico the car had taken me through, I had forgotten the buzz of the great avenues like Reforma and Insurgentes, laid out by Emperor Maximilian in the spirit of Haussman, the architect of nineteenth-century Paris. Every intersection was crowned by a statue, including one to the last Aztec emperor, Cuauhtémoc, and there was a vicious roundabout system in which traffic moved both clockwise and anticlockwise.

The taxi drivers drove Volkswagen Beetles, which honked and buzzed around the Oldsmobile. I hadn't quite mastered the technique of indicators, but then no one else had either. At least I was bigger than them; my 1972 Oldsmobile was the largest and heaviest model of Oldsmobile 98 ever made, and weighed a ton: or two tons to be precise, according to my owner's manual.

I made for a club in the area around the Cuauhtémoc statue, a place called the Peña del Payador where I had spent many happy hours. It was the nearest to a home I'd had in Mexico. The Peña was modelled on the Andean clubs that played the protest folk music of Argentina and of Chile. I had heard pipe-music there of a ferocity to put the muzaked European imitations to shame, as well as angry young men performing the songs of Victor Jara and other Latin American heroes.

Victor Jara was a particular favourite of mine; I had most of his albums. Listening to his sweet-voiced laments about love or going down the mine was a reminder of his cruel death at the hands of Pinochet's Chilean butchers in 1973. He had been such a symbol of Allende's 'new Chile' that Pinochet's men had cut off his hands and then forced him to play to the other prisoners in the football stadium they were using as a concentration camp, before he was summarily killed.

As I had hoped, Jesús was there. As I had also hoped, he invited me to stay with him and his family for a while.

It was good to see him again. Jesús was my age and had the large hooked nose of a Maya and a permanently benign smile. He had been my closest friend in the DF. I told him of my trip down from Texas and he laughed at my boots. 'Midnight cowboy', he called me. The first ten minutes I could hardly get a word out, we were laughing so hard.

There were some boisterous Argentinian singers sitting with Jesús. They had just been to Texas to play for a *latino* audience: 'We sung a song, a song to the light of the moon [long pause for effect], and someone stood up and said, "fuck the light of the moon, we're going there tomorrow!"'

Argentinians were the core audience at the club, many of them exiles from the horrors of the military dictatorship, *la dictadura*. They told stories of bodies being bundled out of plane windows over the sea off Buenos Aires, stories that at the time seemed too fantastical to be true. They had a dangerous edge to them as well, the Argentinians; you never knew which way they were going to jump after a drink or two.

The great issue of the day was the continuing civil war in Nicaragua. When living in the capital before, I had read a paper called *Uno Más Uno* for updates on the war. *Uno Más Uno* had a tough left-wing stance (its line on the boat-people, for instance, was more sympathetic to the Vietnamese government than to the refugees) and it was unsurprising that it should support the Sandinista rebels. But the Mexicans as a whole were sympathetic to the plight of the downtrodden Nicaraguans. The cupidity and brutality of President Somoza were held to be self-evident. Here was a man capable of napalm-bombing his own people, just as he had pocketed most of the international relief sent over after the earthquake that had devastated Managua in 1972.

For the young, you didn't even need to know that; one look at the fat, self-satisfied Somoza, with his empty rhetoric about *la patria*, 'the fatherland', and then at the Sandinista rebels – the dashing Commander Zero, a maverick in a bandana, or their poet Ernesto Cardenal – was enough. The rebels had all the glamour of rock and roll, as The Clash were to exploit some years later, posing in faux combat gear for their *Sandinista* album.

In the Peña, the regulars would murmur occasionally about going down to join the International Brigade. Nothing ever came of it, but it was a good thing to say as you downed your tequila. The fantasy was that you went down, fought with '*los chicos*', got the odd cosmetically enhancing scar and came back to bask in the glory. When we read of the heavy casualties sustained by the Sandinistas (including international volunteers), there was less of such talk.

But it was still a Spanish Civil War – you were either for or against the republicans (the Somozas were like hereditary royalty) and if you were against, what was your problem? The news when I arrived that evening in the Peña was that an American journalist called Bill Stewart had been shot by the Somocistas in front of the world's media: it was thought the resulting uproar might jolt the Americans out of their apathy. Like Pancho Villa and the Pershing raid, Americans would tolerate anything 'south of the border' as long as it didn't involve their nationals. The deaths of thousands of Nicaraguans were as nothing to one lone American.

It was clear that Bill Stewart had died courageously, standing up to soldiers who were abusing civilians. We toasted him in tequila, from the safety of our Mexico City bar.

I headed back with Jesús to his home in the southern suburb. It was a quieter part of the DF, and that way I hoped to avoid police checks. We were stopped within about ten minutes of leaving the club.

'Jesus!' I exclaimed to Jesús (confusingly, but he didn't seem to mind). 'This is all I need!' Apart from anything else, I had been drinking heavily to try and countereffect the carbon monoxide poisoning.

There were two of them. They looked mean.

Cop 1: 'Where are your papers?'

Cop 2: (quoting) 'Turning when not in the correct lane is an *infracción*, fine, of 500 pesos.' He held up a grubby photostatted list.

Cop 1: 'Where are your *placas*, numberplates?'

I produced my temporary cardboard Texan plates from behind the seat and waved them hopefully at him.

Cop 1: 'What the fuck are these? This is more serious.'

The cops started to talk together in a way that made me uneasy 'No conferring,' I wanted to scream. I remembered and used the formal mantra Enrique had taught me in the hills: '*Señores caballeros, ¿no hay otra manera de arreglar la cosa?* Gentlemen, is there no other way we can arrange this matter?'

Jesús gave a strangled moan beside me. Cop 1 (the bigger one) laughed and gave me a pitying look: 'No, *Sir*, there is no fucking way we can "arrange this matter", *Sir*'.

I had forgotten the Mexico City inability to utter the simplest phrase without an expletive; they made the Bronx streets look like Sunday School.

I waved some Mexican money. The other cop made a gesture for me to hold it below the windscreen. He came over and leant in. 'Now if you had any dollars ...' There was a stash in the glove compartment I kept in case the peso made one of its occasional lurches in value. I peeled off a few sorely needed green notes, my reserve.

'Put them in your driving licence and hand over your licence.'

'I don't have my licence on me.'

'Why the fuck not? ¡*Chingada Madre*! Motherfucker! All right, give me the fucking money and get out of here!'

Shaken and considerably stirred, we made it back to Jesús's house. Jesús wasn't happy. 'Hugo, if you want to stay in the DF, you're going to have to get a licence.'

*

Now, more than ever, I did indeed need to stay in Mexico City if I was to earn enough money to get me through the rest of the country. The next day we went to the offices of the transport authority, an imposing building in the centre of Mexico City.

It would be an understatement to say that I was worried. The traffic outside the authority was swirling with the usual ferocity. I had the official booklet with hundreds of complicated Mexican road signs. My only previous experience of a driving test, back in England, had not been a happy experience. Perhaps unwisely, I had drunk a pint or two beforehand to help me through the ordeal, and it had made my driving over-emphatic. Nor could I remember half the signs. The tester had covered my scoresheet in crosses.

Things didn't start well here either. 'I don't like the colour of your eyes,' said the clerk, when I handed in my form. I thought I had misheard him, although, confusingly, Mexicans did often talk to me about my eyes, and how blue they were compared to what they described as their own *ojos de cafe*, 'coffee-coloured' ones.

Jesús knew what to do. 'How much will it cost him as a fine for having the wrong colour eyes?' he said wearily. We reached a figure and handed it over in cash. The clerk cheered up and did triplicate copies of the form, rounded off with an emphatic green stamp.

Outside, the man supposed to conduct the test looked similar to his English counterpart, large and reeking of competence and authority, with one noticeable difference: he had a gun the size of an elephant's testicle dangling from his belt. There was a Volkswagen Rabbit at the side of the road. I began to panic as I went to get in. He held me back. 'No, no. Let's talk for a minute. ¿*Tiene cigarro*? Cigarette?'

I gave him one. We chatted about the weather and the forthcoming elections. I kept on my guard in case he slipped in a casual question about parking procedures or what to do in an emergency stop, but it never came.

On finishing the cigarette, he congratulated me. I had passed the test. 'If anyone asks, remember that you took it in a Volkswagen Rabbit, that there were dual-control pedals in the car and that we took fifteen minutes.' He saw me do a double take, waved the papers the clerk had stamped and smiled. 'This is because you have priority status.' It was a one-stop bribe system.

It was a good feeling to know that I was now a legitimate driver, with my own plastic-coated driving licence. The only worry was that everybody else in Mexico City had got their licences the same way.

One day I watched at a crossroads as two cars converged from opposite directions. They both slowed to a crawl, but neither man wanted to give ground. One advanced, then the other, with a lot of horn-blowing and *mal ojo*, giving the other guy the eye. Finally they gave a last lurch at the same time and collided. I laughed. They got out and started shouting at each other.

Mexico City was said to be the only city in the world where

drivers would speed up when they saw pedestrians ahead. Most of the time I garaged the Oldsmobile around Jesús's home. His large, extended family lived in the suburb of Tasqueña and it was a joy to stay with them. His five brothers and sisters all seemed to share Jesús's warm, smiling view of life, as well as having the large family nose – which may have caused problems as two of the sisters were having operations for sinusitis. Jesús's father ran a small family business of some sort (I could never quite discover what), which Jesús helped with occasionally, while his mother presided over proceedings with quiet calm, dispensing *tamales* and sympathy.

There was an uncle who stayed with the family called Pablo. He was only five feet tall, with an evil glint in his eye and a meticulous moustache; he wore leather jackets to make himself look bigger. Jesús told me at times he would disappear for drinking sprees, only to re-emerge days later.

The first time I met him was early one evening when he came back from just such a bout. I was impressed that anyone could be finishing that early – it showed he had been going right through from the previous night.

Jesús and I were watching a TV documentary on Nicaragua and Pablo slumped on a chair. He fell asleep for a while. At one point he woke up and started crying: 'No puedo seguir más, I can't go on any further.' Jesús ignored him. When at last he woke up and realised who I was, he came out fighting: 'Fucking English,' he said, 'fucking English, you're nothing but *piratas. ¡Drago!*' He spat. It took a while for me to realise he was talking about Sir Francis Drake.

Jesús's little brother Demetrio laughed. This infuriated Pablo. He stood up and swayed over me. 'Show me you're a man then,' he said. 'We'll have a chilli-eating contest.'

'¡*No*! ¡*No*! ¡*No*!' cried Jesús, who had clearly been through this before. 'Pablito, you don't need to do this.'

But Pablo was determined. He went to the kitchen and came back with a range of the chillies that Jesús's mother, like all Mexican cooks, kept in a perpetual state of readiness: the conventional mild types that come over to England, but also little pod chillies that seemed to get stronger the smaller they were, and some *habanero* chillies, the so-called 'crying chillies of Yucatan', that could deprive a grown man of his breath.

Jesús got out some beers, lined up a parallel row of chillies and we set off. I tried to lighten the tone by talking about English mustard and how strong it was, how it must be good training for this sort of event, but Pablo was having none of this. 'Go on gringo, just eat the fucking chillies,' he shouted.

The rest of the family came in, attracted by the noise, and it became something of a circus. After I had nibbled delicately on a few milder red ones, trying to keep to the middles as the tips were stronger, the crowd whooped me on. The danger lay in the fatal moment's delay between the bite and the implosive shock on the taste buds, a delay that fooled me into going straight on to a second exploratory bite. It was like having elastoplast stripped from the roof of your mouth.

The good news was that Pablo was making even heavier weather of it than me. I hated to think what the raw chillies were contending with when they got down to his stomach; from his breath I guessed that there was enough liquid alcohol sloshing around below for his innards to go up like a paraffin stove. Just before we reached the *habanero* chillies, he threw in the towel. In fact he went to the bathroom and threw rather more than that copiously into the toilet.

That Sunday we all went off for a day trip to Amecameca, a

market town to the south of the city, for a long, rambling lunch at a Spanish restaurant. Jesús's father, who originally came from Veracruz, told me a string of impenetrable Gulf Coast jokes at which I laughed politely.

Then we drove to the base of Popocatépetl, the large volcano that dominates the Valley of Mexico, together with its 'female' and more softly contoured counterpart Ixtaccíhuatl. There was a small road that went up the Paso de Cortés, the pass between these volcanoes that the conquistadors used to approach Tenochtitlán – Mexico City as was – in 1519. I was pleased to see the statue of Cortés at the top of the pass, looking out over the valley he was coming to conquer; I had heard that this was the only statue of him in the entire country (although as Evelyn Waugh had pointed out, this was perhaps not surprising – there are no statues to Julius Caesar in Britain, whatever the virtues of Roman rule).

It must have been an extraordinary moment for Cortés. After having been led by his Indian guides on a circuitous route from the coast, he was finally within reach of the city he had heard so much about. Coming over the pass was a bold and unexpected move too: at 10,000 feet, it was not the easy way to approach the Aztec capital.

But then Cortés was a much maligned figure. The letters he sent back to the emperor Charles V, and the accounts of his contemporaries like Bernal Díaz, reveal him to be a thoughtful and engaged commander, capable of just such bold strokes as taking the Paso de Cortés; the earlier destruction of his boats – and therefore means of retreat – at Veracruz being just another example.

Not given to gambling, drink or unnecessary slaughter, his one weakness seems to have been for women. He broke a leg in one youthful escapade in Spain when crawling over roofs to get to his paramour, and chased everything in a Spanish or Indian skirt when he got to Mexico.

The Spaniards impressed the Aztecs here by sending a few men up the volcano to gather some lava – supposedly for gunpowder, but more likely, given Cortés's cunning psychology, to show they were not afraid of the smoking mountain in the way the indigenous peoples were.

Popocatépetl certainly looked like a volcano should look, with the upturned funnel of a classical Japanese woodcut. Perhaps fuelled by our extended and liquid Sunday lunch, I was determined to climb it.

'How about it?' I said to Jesús.

He smiled: '¿*Cómo no*? Why not?'

So the next weekend we found ourselves sleeping in the refuge hut on the mountain. The hut lay at an altitude of 13,000 feet and there were some further 5,000 feet to get to the top. From my limited experience of climbing in the Lake District or Snowdonia, I knew two things about mountains: that it got bloody cold and that you were supposed to start early. Compared to the other climbers in the hut, we were, to say the least, unprepared. They were mostly European, big, blonde and handsome; there was a lot of manly talk about altitude acclimatisation and how useful crampons and ice-axes were. By comparison, Jesús and I in our cheap boots and layers of jerseys (some supplied by Jesús's sisters, so pink) must have looked like punk waifs.

On getting up at what seemed the unearthly hour of seven o'clock, I was surprised to find that all the other parties of climbers had already set off. Jesús was snoring as only someone with a nose the size of a boomerang could. I kicked him awake and we heated up some refried beans Jesús's mother had given us before leaving.

The clouds were already below the refuge, so the mountain

stood out in perfect relief. I had never seen clouds below me before, except from a plane. We could see other parties ahead of us in small groups of neon yellow or orange, but they were making slow progress. When we reached the start of the climb, we realised why: for every two steps forward, you slid back a foot in the thick volcanic dust.

In a naïve way, I had expected there to be some sort of track to follow, but it was soon clear that it was every man for himself. We started a long, slow assault up the scree and the dust to reach a ridge called Querétano, where there was a yellow, triangular hut. By the time we got there, the clouds had started to rise. It was bitingly cold. Inside the hut we found one of the 'pro' groups of Europeans we had seen the night before, two Dutch men and a girl, and also some Mexicans, one of whom turned out to be a bullfighter. I had some brandy in a hip flask that Jesús's father had lent me, which went down well with the Mexicans but not the Dutch, who sniffed about dehydration.

It gave us heart for the next leg up beside a glacier and small waterfall, in the shadow of a large outcrop of rock called la Muela, the Molar. We crested a series of ridges and the going got hard: I seemed to be on all fours for longer than was either dignified or effective. Meanwhile Jesús had settled into the determined plod of a man who is going to get to the top no matter what; I lagged behind him like a mule after its master, hoping that his pace would help me up.

We came over a rise to see two monumental ridges ahead of us that looked as if they had been hewn from the stone as a temple for an Aztec deity like Quetzalcoatl; for one brief moment brought on by hypoxia and stupidity, I thought they actually had been carved. Just beyond them was the snowline and what looked like the remains of another refuge.

I had lugged a bottle of red wine up with me, and we reviewed the situation over disgusting cold swigs of frozen tannin and some bread rolls. It had taken us five or six hours to get this far. The clouds were now rising higher and higher below us. Nor did we have a map or compass. 'Let's go on,' said Jesús with all the confidence of a man who has never been on a mountain in his life and is not going to let that stop him.

We started up the snow, but it had started to compact into sheet ice. It was hopeless. Quite how Cortés's men had managed in all their armour, I couldn't think. Maybe they had lied. Nor could we see the top from where we were, which was dispiriting. 'Discretion is the better part of valour,' I translated to Jesús. He was tickled pink by the phrase. We decided we were beaten. After all if Che Guevera had been unable to get to the top on his first attempt, we were in good company. Che had left a good account:

I took Popocatépetl by assault, but despite much heroism, I was unable to reach the top. I was ready to die for it, but my Cuban climbing companion scared me because two of his toes froze . . . We spent six hours fighting the snow that buried us to our waist, and with feet totally drenched since we lacked the proper equipment. The guide got lost in the fog skirting a crevasse, and we were exhausted from the soft and unending snow. The Cubans won't climb again, but for me, as soon as I have some money, I will challenge the Popo again . . .

(letter to his mother, July 20, 1955)

We went down a different way, by what appeared to be a short cut but soon turned into a morass of dust and sharp defiles. When we got to a good scree slope, we could slide down the stones, but then it was back to trudging through more volcanic dust. By now we were extremely cold and taking large gulps of the brandy to warm us up. After traversing a long ridge that seemed to lead us away from our original route, we crossed a dry stream bed where the water had washed away the dust to reveal a beautiful mosaic of red and blue volcanic stone. Then the cloud came up and covered us completely.

Jesús was a good man for a crisis. 'Well we can't go wrong if we just head straight down, surely?' The logic seemed impeccable, even if it meant ripping my threadbare trousers to pieces on the rocks below.

It was with relief that we saw some professional neon jackets threading along below us; we emerged on top of the Dutch party, to their evident surprise. Their leader studied his map. 'That is not a route you have just come down,' he pronounced, categorically.

Safely back in Mexico City we ate heavily spiced prawn soup and allowed ourselves to be fêted by the women of Jesús's family. For days my face had an altitude burn from the wind and the sun.

*

I needed to get some money. Ramón, the cheerful drug dealer who frequented the Peña, offered me some part-time work selling dope to the many American foreign-language students living around Mexico City. He had an elaborate system of commission worked out, where I would have worked on an increasing scale of commission by volume of sale, like an Avon lady; I figured it was complicated enough having an illegal car without stuffing it full of drugs as well.

Instead I got work at a bank as a translator and all-round gopher.

The bank was a development bank, funded by an international consortium and giving loans to Mexican businesses in what they liked to style 'benevolent' venture capitalism. This sounded a contradiction in terms, but as the money sounded good I wasn't going to get funny about it. The real problem for the Mexican businesses the bank lent money to was that the loans were always in American dollars; as their earnings were in pesos, they were often held hostage by the frequent collapse in the exchange rate.

My boss's name was Julio. The first day, Julio took me out to lunch and explained the principles behind doing successful business in Mexico. Everyone worked from ten until two. An extended lunch would then go on for hours, sometimes until five in the afternoon, before everybody headed back to the office until eight in the evening.

Lunch was the real work. 'Our business depends largely on trust,' said Julio. 'The idea is that Mexicans can only trust one another when they are so drunk they are almost blind. So in this bank we always drink Tequila Oils before we begin any negotiations.'

I prided myself on having drunk tequila most of the ways it came – from classic Margaritas to the dark 'Comemerativo' that looked more like whisky. I had even sunk to the depths of the abominable Sunrise and all sorts of sugary variations. But I had never heard of a Tequila Oil.

Julio gave an order to the waiter. He came back with a double tequila mixed with tomato juice. I didn't like the look of it (tomatoes belonged with vodka), but it still seemed plausible. Then Julio took a large tablespoon of the *habanero* chilli sauce that was on the table and ostentatiously mixed it in. Other diners were beginning to watch him. He took a bottle of black Maggi out of his briefcase. I had seen the stuff in European restaurants, a sharp, aromatic version of HP sauce. He stirred enough in to turn the drink black and viscous. It did indeed look like oil.

'Try this Hugito. Just as the alcohol hits your stomach, the chilli will as well and blow it back into your brain. It will take your head off.'

It did.

So began a memorable set of serious lunches. Julio and I would turn up at a factory, fence around the issues with the bosses and then go out to one of the many wonderful restaurants in the city. We would order dried ants in chocolate or *mole poblano*, the great national dish of dried chillies, turkey and chocolate, or smoked peppers in a walnut sauce ('¡*Ricísimo!*' the maître d' would murmur appreciatively as he took our order). Julio would get out his mixing kit, line up three or four of his Tequila Oils in front of everyone at the table and within half an hour we would all be friends for life and have a sensibly renegotiated loan.

Julio had one favourite phrase whenever we finished off a negotiation: 'Hey,' he would say, spreading his arms wide and laughing, 'it's not my money, after all.' Which would be a cue for drinks all round.

We visited a furniture factory where they made, among other things, cinema seats. A machine simulated a pair of rotating buttocks that was used to test wear on the cushions. Any fabric had to be able to withstand so many thousand simulated buttock undulations before being passed suitable for cinema use. The machine even swivelled both ways to take account of variations in individual buttock movements.

It was a family business and we headed round the corner afterwards to a restaurant where, they assured us, the patron had a particular treat in store. 'You've heard of the worm at the bottom of the mezcal bottle, Hugo.' I had indeed often made its acquaintance, although I had never been far gone enough to eat it. 'Well this is a dish of raw worms that have been soaked in mezcal before being cooked.' I gulped slightly. They all looked at me. As so often in Mexico, I realised that this was a test. I knocked back a Tequila Oil to help me through the coming ordeal.

The worms came with a tortilla wrapped around them, as a taco, so at least you couldn't see them. Commending myself to the Virgin of Guadalupe, I bit into the taco as enthusiastically as I could. The worms were big chunky ones that had been deep-fried to give them a sort of crunchy texture that was not disagreeable. Guacamole also helped disguise the taste.

'Bring me more,' I cried.

'*Ándale*,' said my host enthusiastically: '¡*Qué cabrón*! What a goat!'

To compensate for the ordeal, a rose-petal pie came for dessert that was the nearest to ambrosia I had ever experienced.

It was with a shock that I read shortly afterwards a poem one of the last of the Aztecs had written after the bitter siege of Tenochtitlán (Mexico City) by the Spaniards:

> Worms writhe along the streets and gathering places
> and the walls are stained with brains.
> The waters are red, as if they had been dyed,
> and if we drink from them, the water is fetid.
> We strike out at the walls of our houses in our grief:
> we inherited much;
> all that we will leave behind is a net of holes.
>
> Our shields were our defence
> but our shields could not prevent our desolation.
> We have eaten rotten food.

We have eaten salty grain.
We have eaten bits of mud, lizards, rats
and the earth made dust.
We have even eaten the worms.

I found it impossible to forget the conquest, not least because the Mexicans never allowed you to. It was a drama that was being constantly replayed, a drama in which the nation had always been wronged by the invader; worse, Cortés had been helped in his conquest by a treacherous female, the Malinche, who became both his translator and mistress. Beside this treachery, the heroic resistance of Cuauhtémoc, the very last Aztec emperor who succeeded the spineless Moctezuma, was held up as the epitome of Mexican stoicism.

There was much that could be questioned about Cuauhtémoc's true heroism. On his ascension to the throne after Montezuma's death, he committed his people to a hopeless final siege and unnecessary suffering when defeat was already inevitable. But at least he also had a sense of humour. When, together with his close follower, the Lord of Tacuba, he was being tortured by the Spaniards, Tacuba complained to his emperor of the pain he was experiencing. 'Well I'm not lying on a bed of flowers myself,' was Cuauhtémoc's famous response.

Nor could I forget, however, Bernal Díaz's account of seeing his Spanish colleagues dragged to their deaths, when their flesh was eaten by the Aztecs 'with a sauce of peppers and tomatoes'. In five hundred years, no one had written a better book about Mexico than Bernal Díaz's *The Conquest of New Spain* – and yet he had written it forty years after the events he describes took place. His eye for detail was extraordinary. How many other narrators would have remembered that on the death of one of their companions, the astrologer Botello, they had opened his belongings and found he had a 4-inch leather dildo stuffed with flock?

The Aztec priests, or '*papas*' as Díaz used to call them, would dose themselves with magic mushrooms to get closer to their gods. This seemed a more pleasurable way of doing it than the Maya trick of sticking hallucinogenic thorns into the penis. Montezuma, who had been a priest himself, took large doses of magic mushrooms, and this may have been part of the reason for his vacillation in the face of the arrival of an enemy who, while determined, could easily have been defeated with a bit of resolution, given Mexica numbers. Like the old hippy joke about the man who had to have a spliff before thinking about what to do next, the mushrooms cannot have helped him deal rationally with invaders who were thought to be living gods returning over the seas.

One Aztec described the reaction of his people when Cortés and his *conquistadores* arrived 'as if everyone had eaten stupefying mushrooms, as if they had seen something astonishing. Terror dominated everyone, as if all the world were being disembowelled. People went to sleep in terror.'

I still fancied some magic mushrooms myself. Jesús and I went to see a film about Maria Sabina, the old wise woman of the hills near Oaxaca. It was after reading an anthropological paper on her in the UCLA libraries that the young Carlos Castaneda had supposedly made the journey south in search of peyote that led him to Don Juan; the jury was still out on whether his books were inspired fiction or fraudulent journalism – and whether it mattered.

However fictional Don Juan might have been, Maria Sabina was all too solidly real, indeed substantially overweight. The film was suitably po-faced as she recounted where the *niños santos*, the 'holy children' as she called the mushrooms, had taken her. There were many shots of her standing by waterfalls in the cloud-valleys of Oaxaca (pronounced 'huar-hacker'). Most of her rituals seemed to combine the pre-Columbian with Christianity in a way that was predictable but oddly moving – a plastic Virgin Mary next to a wooden Tlaloc, the Aztec god of rain.

She recounted to the camera in a matter-of-fact way what had happened during one prolonged mushroom session. After various traumatic confrontations with eagles and jaguars, she had finally come to a place of death, the place at the end of it all, where, in her words, 'one finds only God . . . and Benito Juárez'. We laughed. Benito Juárez, Mexico's first pure-blooded Indian president after Independence, enjoyed near universal reverence.

I pestered Ramón, the drug dealer, to get some mushrooms for me. He was reluctant as, like Fernando back in Chihuahua, he thought mushrooms were strictly Indian. '¡*Pendejo!*', he told me, 'you stupid bastard, keep to the real thing. Why can't you just buy marijuana like everybody else?'

He finally came up with some from Zautla, a small town on the way to Veracruz, which Ramón passed when he did a regular collection run to the port. They grew naturally there and this may well have been the region Montezuma and his priests obtained them from, not the more famous Oaxaca. On principle, Ramón refused to take any money for them. 'I only sell stuff where I can guarantee satisfaction, *Hugito.* Just like Coca-Cola do. And this stuff could be *mierda*, shit, for all I know.'

They came in a small paper bag. I put them in my jacket and took a bus down towards Jesús's house. Waiting by the road for my next connection, I studied them with care. They looked dull and uninteresting.

I had once read a story by P. G. Wodehouse in which a man was despatched by his girlfriend to find strawberries in winter as a test of his affection. After a series of the usual Wodehousian adventures (stealing policemen's helmets, up before magistrates, staying with difficult aunts etc.), he managed to get hold of some of the precious fruit and rushed with them to the house of said girlfriend, who was still dressing upstairs. As he waited for her to come down, he thought he had better test the strawberries for quality. The first one tasted pretty good. So did the last.

The same happened to me. I had meant to share them with Jesús, but curiosity got the better. Besides which, the first two or three didn't seem to do much, so I thought I would be doing Jesús a favour if I got rid of the lot. There were about a dozen.

Ten minutes later, I was still waiting for that bus. Nothing had happened. Another ten minutes and the bus came. I put down my *Hermelinda* comic (I had acquired a taste for her morbid antics) and tried to cross the pavement. Whoooohay. The pavement was crossing over me. Time to regroup.

There was a fairground over the way and I staggered inside, thinking I would be less conspicuous. The mushrooms seemed to be settling down. There were no hallucinations, just an intense adjusting of colours, light and sound, as if someone had fiddled with my control knobs. I was having a great time. There were a couple of girls hanging around by a taco stand who, on reflection, may have been looking for casual trade. They noticed me lurching around in my cowboy boots. 'Hey cowboy,' they giggled, 'can you shoot?' There was a rifle-range near by.

Was this really a good idea, I wondered, as the thickset *macizo* of a Mexican handed me the gun? I needn't have worried. My eyesight, myopic at the best of times, seemed to have acquired super-sensitive precision. I hit everything and won a bunch of large pink cuddly toys with bits of candy floss coming out of their ears, which I gallantly handed to the girls. 'You're all very beautiful,' I told them.

I left them to head on to the next attraction. It was a type of big wheel I had never seen before: there were no seats and you were strapped instead against the walls. I felt I could handle it. The power of the mushrooms came in waves, so there were reassuring pauses in psychic activity where it all quietened down, like a jacuzzi being turned on and off. What I hadn't realised was that once the wheel got going, it turned upright and horizontal. The only thing that stopped you from dropping through the strap was centrifugal force as it spun round at ever increasing speed.

Even on a good day, it would have been an experience. With a dozen magic mushrooms rattling around inside me, my head started to open up like a Leonardo cartoon. I started shouting and screaming and they had to stop the wheel to get me off. I hadn't got to see God or Benito Juárez, but I had been close enough for the experience to have been uncomfortable.

Jesús laughed at me when I finally got to the house, looking distinctly the worse for wear. '¡*No puedo seguir más!*' he cried, imitating Pablo's 'I can't go on!' I decided to stick to alcohol.

*

At work, Julio insisted I buy a suit with my first pay packet; at least I could defy office conventions by also wearing the caribou cowboy boots. My role was a curious one: there never seemed much translating to do (technically, I was supposed to write a report in English on each of the clients we visited), but it was useful to have someone around the office who could write a report in English to any overseas backers that was as opaque as the dense Mexican style.

I found myself taking the Metro every day from Jesús's house, just like a regular commuter. There was a terrific sign on the carriages to sort out the wise guys: 'It is forbidden to smoke or to hold a lighted cigarette in the hand.' There were a lot of wise guys. They had forcibly to segregate the sexes coming out of the big stations because there was so much groping: males to the left, women to the right.

One day an old man got talking to me. There was no preamble. He just leant over and said right up close: 'Women like to be dominated. They like to feel the man has the upper hand. They are more intelligent than us, of course, but they are passive. Don't you think?'

I didn't think much of this, as I told him. Punk orthodoxy, and the view among most of my English friends at the time, male or female, was that the sexes were essentially the same emotionally; they just happened to have different body parts attached. It was curious to be in a culture that still held the two to be different species cohabiting out of necessity.

There was a pretty secretary in the office called Mina, with chestnut hair cut to an Audrey Hepburn gamine fringe, and we started to walk out together in a genteel sort of way. She was funny about the office and its small inconsequentialities. We would go to the movies or eat at Sanborns or VIPS, American style restaurants with reassuring menus of hamburgers and chips alongside the tacos. I plumped unapologetically for the hamburgers; I had eaten enough tacos and refried beans to last a lifetime.

We went to the races. The Hippodrome had a beautiful tree-lined approach and an ornamental lake. As we cruised up in the Oldsmobile, which I had cleaned to impress Mina, I felt pretty good. The simple pleasures were the best, I thought: a pretty girl, a sunny day and the racetrack. What could be better?

We looked respectable, with me in a suit and Mina in a cocktail dress; the doorman offered to get us into the reserved members' enclosure for a small *descuento* (literally 'discount', but in fact the reverse – a hefty bribe). I found myself bribing with considerable enjoyment now, or as much as one ever could when parting from money. There was a certain complicity, like sharing a drink from the same bottle.

The enclosure looked over a bright, sunny amphitheatre, with the hills beyond; the centre of the track had been carefully filled with ornamental flower beds. My memory of British racetracks was of floors covered in dirt and discarded hot-dog wrappers. This was more salubrious. Helped by the sunshine, the colours of the jockeys were reflected in the bright shirts and dresses of the prosperous members' enclosure.

There was a substantial minimum drinks charge per head, so people were getting their money's worth and ordering doubles of everything. Mina didn't drink much, so I drank hers too.

A nice old boy in a bright-yellow cashmere scarf explained the betting system of *quinelas* to us. He gave me precisely the same hoary old advice about how to spot a winner I had heard at Chepstow or Cheltenham. I had my own simpler system: just as you should always buy a car for its colour (the electric blue of the Oldsmobile), so you should always pick a horse by its name. I went for Manos Llenas, 'Hands Full', at 9-2 each way. The odds seemed cautious, so I compensated by putting in a good wedge of my last pay cheque.

Miraculously, it came through by the final circuit and was leading the pack. Mina and I started screaming and holding each other. The table next door checked with us that it was our horse and started screaming for us as well. Then it dropped into second. I squeezed Mina even harder. Just at the line, it got pipped into third. I gave Mina a final hug, but this time she drew away.

This was the thing with her and for that matter with our whole relationship. We went through some of the rituals of *noviazgo*, the long indolent courtship of Mexican couples, like boating on Chapultepec Park or going to the movies, but anything further, anything more physical, was out.

This wasn't out of any ignorance or timidity – Mina, like most of the Mexican girls I had met, had as filthy a mind as anything. She was fond of making jokes about chillies; the Mexicans always equated them with their obvious anatomical counterpart and jokes about *chupar el chile*, 'chilli-sucking', or how hot someone's chilli was, were legion.

Nor was there a fierce father, or worse mother, waiting up at night with a shotgun for any potential suitors; it was just *una cosa de respeto*, 'a thing of respect' for Mina, the way she felt about herself. However, she did talk to me one night of how much she hated the whole rigidity of virginity and that hers, she felt, was surely the last generation who would keep so canonically to it.

The whole thing was a little embarrassing. She was all of twenty-eight, some ten years older than me; I would have been laughed off the streets back in England. And her friends said that I was *pan de mañana*, 'tomorrow's bread'. But she was pretty and I was as lecherous as only an eighteen-year-old with some money in his pocket can be, so it was frustrating that holding hands and the odd chaste kiss were about as far as it ever got.

I still enjoyed her company; we would play Turista, a Mexican version of Monopoly, or go down to Xochimilco, the last of the old Aztec water-gardens that remained, where we drifted around on canoes looking at the lilies floating on the water.

*

The car was getting me into trouble. Around Jesús's house the police had a nasty habit of setting traps on the lights. As they had access to the control boxes (supposedly to switch them off if there was an accident), they could cut down the length of time the lights were on amber. You might set off across a junction on green, but by the time you got to the other side, there would be a red light and helpful police car waiting for you. Out would come the photostatted list of '*infracciones*' and a suitable bribe would be needed. I paid extra for the dubious distinction of being both a gringo and having no numberplates. The suburban police weren't as venal as the ones in the centre of the city, but it was getting me down.

One night I went off to pick Mina up to see a movie. The radio was on and there was one of those fine Mexico City sunsets that the smog causes, where the mountains get rimmed in different colours of nitrous red. I turned into the big Churubusco avenue still singing along to the radio. There was a Barry White song playing and I was a closet fan, although I had never been able to admit this to my friends.

The oncoming car hit me with a sickening thud right in the centre of the junction, and the Oldsmobile gave a horrible lurch, like a frightened horse, before it cannonballed back. Either I had misread a light and gone straight into the incoming traffic, or the police had fiddled once too often with the junction-box controls. The moulding on the side of the car was whipping back off the stoved-in side panels of the car and making a horrible whining noise as I slewed over onto the curb.

I turned round to try to see the other car. It was behind me, with the driver gesticulating. A whole family were beside him, looking shocked.

Sweat broke out all over me. I had no insurance and I knew

what the Mexican policy on such cases was – throw the parties in prison until the paperwork was resolved.

The man driving demanded my passport. I refused to give it to him. I did immediately hand over all that I had on me in cash, $100. I couldn't see the damage very clearly in the half-light and in the shock of it all, but it looked considerable.

'It's not enough. Follow me to the Delegación, the police station,' he said, '*pueden arreglar todo*, they can arrange everything.'

I followed close behind his car until we came to the exit off the big *Periférico* dual carriageway. My adrenalin was pumping. As he indicated to get off, I followed to the last minute but then veered away and stayed on the carriageway when he was committed to the sliproad. I knew he couldn't get back onto the carriageway without lengthy acrobatics. I hit the Oldsmobile accelerator with a vengeance. I had never driven so fast. The crash might have crunched in half the bodywork, but it hadn't affected the engine. When I was miles along the carriageway, I pulled off and stopped in a side-street. I was still shaking as I got out of the car and had a piss against the wall in the light of the headlights.

It had not been a heroic action. I felt there was only one thing I could do to salvage my self-respect: still go and see the movie.

Mina was taken aback when I arrived with the Oldsmobile ripped to shreds, but she asked surprisingly few questions; it was one of the many things I liked about her. Also, there wasn't much time before the movie started. Ironically the film was *Blue Collar*, about an American car factory.

It was time to leave Mexico City. Even on a deliberately drifting schedule, I had been lured too long by the city of thieves and princes. I went to see Saúl, the mechanic with the split lip living opposite Jesús, who had already done some necessary repairs to the car when I arrived in the DF.

'*Putamadre*, mother of all whores,' he said, 'what happened to the *lancha?*' Saúl, Jesús and the other guys on the block always referred to my car as the *lancha*, the 'land yacht'. There was a lot of head-scratching. I did not have much money as my lifestyle in the DF had not been frugal.

Saúl proposed that if I helped with the bodywork, particularly the spray-painting, he would accept my camera as part-payment, along with a reduced fee. This was a good deal as my camera was a Russian Zenith, the cheapest camera on the market back in Britain, and built like a Soviet tank without the finesse. Even better, Saúl would accept a delay in payment until I came back with the camera after selling the car in Central America. 'I trust you,' said Saúl. This touched me. I would never have trusted myself.

I talked to Julio at the bank. He had a good idea.

'Hugo, do you know how to play golf?'

'No. I hate golf. People in blazers play it.'

'Never mind, it will still work. I need someone to manage a golf course. And it will get you out of the DF.'

One of the bank's clients had defaulted badly, caught out by the most recent dollar-exchange collapse, and as collateral the bank was receiving a prestigious golf club in Cuernavaca. They needed someone to baby-sit the place until they could find a proper buyer. I got excited. I wanted to go to Cuernavaca anyway. It was also (vaguely) south, so I was still heading in the right direction.

Jesús's mother made me up a hamper of food, Jesús's father lent me some money and I was set to go. I was overwhelmed by their hospitality and by the knowledge that any poor Mexican adrift in Britain would be lucky to get directions, let alone such warm and unstinting support.

I had a final meal with Mina at the Casa de los Azulejos, the

'House of Tiles', a sumptuously decorated old colonial restaurant. It was a strange meal, as a leave-taking on a relationship that had never really happened, and so both of us were perhaps more honest than usual. Mina told me again of her despair of being in 'a battle-scarred generation' of Catholic women who, while casual sex was practised all around them, stuck heroically to their guns.

Then we walked across the endless space of the nearby Zócalo, the main square and the centre of the country, from where presidents made long speeches on Independence Day with rolling rhetorical cadences; Spanish lends itself to rhetoric easily, with all its dull but statuesque words pregnant with supposed implication. The Zócalo was so out-of-scale compared to the neighbouring streets because it had been the main square of the Aztecs' city. The Spaniards had demolished all the surrounding buildings, but kept this central plaza.

Just the previous year, there had been great excitement when they had discovered the remains of some of these Aztec pyramids in one corner of the Zócalo, which they were now excavating. I disliked the whole business of pyramid worship that everyone colluded in, from tourists to the whole 'military-heritage complex' that dominated Mexican government. The governing PRI, the *Partido Revolucionario Institucional*, used the pre-Columbian past as ready-made Stalinist artifacts that could forever proclaim the heroic resistance of the 'true' Mexican people to the invader. The dubious historical line was that the Mexican Revolution had finally returned the power to the Mexican people that the Aztecs had lost. The current PRI president, López Portillo, had even written a book about Quetzalcoatl.

The villain of the ancient Aztec world was a 'grand vizier' called Tlacaelel, who nominally served under four successive Aztec emperors during the key phase of their brief hundred-year reign of superiority, but wielded the real power. One of his first and most significant acts was to rewrite the Aztecs' past: the 'old books' recounting their true history as just one wandering tribe among many were burnt. Instead Tlacaelel instigated the convenient political myth that they were directly descended from the Toltecs, a previous race whose substantial ruins could still be seen near the Valley of Mexico. This gave them the genealogical pretensions to go with their territorial ambitions.

Under Tlacaelel's direction, the warrior god Huitzilopochtli was elevated from minor to major player in the complicated pantheon of gods, and had to be propitiated with ever increasing amounts of victims. Human sacrifice, which had previously been a rare and sporadic accompaniment to ritual festivals, became a growth industry, with the priests becoming ever more powerful.

When the pyramid that was now being excavated had first been inaugurated, in 1487, there were prisoners lined up for sacrifice stretching in all directions as far as the eye could see. Twenty thousand victims were killed in a single day.

The smell and stench of blood at such mass ceremonies must have been nauseous. While the heart itself would have been burnt, each skull was collected on a skull-rack with all the book-keeping pedantry of Mexicans; the rest of the body was flung down the steps of the pyramid, to be eaten later with chilli sauce by nobles or favoured warriors.

Tlacaelel devised different ways of killing victims. In addition to the usual cutting of the heart from the live body while the victim was bent over a sacrificial stone, he started to burn them alive as well.

The self-perpetuating waging of wars to obtain more sacrificial victims for the success of yet further wars meant that the Aztecs exploded from obscurity to military dominance as spectacularly as the Third Reich – and for many of their conquered territories, the experience must have been similar to Nazi occupation: their people and children taken for sacrifice to Tenochtitlán, a city of death, as Tlacaelel harangued his people into ever greater conquest. 'We are capable of conquering the entire world,' he told a neighbouring king, Goebbels-style.

Tlacaelel was long departed by the time the conquistadors arrived, but his baleful legacy of a theocracy driven by fear and bloodshed lived on. In that sense, Cortés's arrival was one of the best things that ever happened to Mexico, even if the Spaniards were often brutal in their own turn and brought disease with them.

I had seen the great stone of Coyolxauhqui in the Anthropology Museum the government had lavished money on as the country's 'patrimony'. It was a beautiful, intricately carved stone to the moon goddess. However, I couldn't help thinking of the bodies that would have tumbled onto it as it lay at the bottom of the pyramid to receive them. There was something obscene in the way that it now stood clean and pristine under the museum's spotlight; its sheer beauty was offensive.

The Mexican writer Octavio Paz single-handedly helped define the Mexican national character in his book *The Labyrinth of Solitude*; he suggested the line that most Mexican and Western intellectuals have followed since – that the Aztec sacrifices should be accepted as just part of a greater whole, and anyway, doesn't all 'history have the cruel reality of a nightmare', a poetic phrase and a disclaimer of any moral responsibility for how that history is remembered.

Mina and I went on from the pyramids to the Plaza Garibaldi a few blocks away, a fun, riotous square where couples went to be serenaded by those prototypical Mexicans, the mariachi musicians: you could hire them to play for you there on the spot or to serenade outside your beloved's window. That evening they were out in force, bustling around in their brocade and paunches: their traditional *traje de charro*, a waist-length jacket with tight, tapered trousers, was not always suited to the fuller figure. One magnificent moustachioed *caporal* of his *banda* was so resplendent in a salmon-coloured suit with silver filigree down his trouser legs that he outshone the rest.

The trumpets were playing, there was a smell of tacos and *mole* in the air, and young couples were dancing slowly in the middle of the square; I felt a wave of emotion as I danced with Mina. There was nothing like leaving to make you realise how much you liked someone.

Then we drank *ponchos*, tequila with fruit and walnuts, in the venerable Tenampa bar near by, the Grand Ole Opry House of the mariachis, an eighty-year-old shrine to their traditions, with pictures of old maestros like Agustín Lara on the walls and almost a mariachi band to every table. We didn't need to pay for any ourselves, as a spendthrift at the next-door table had got them lined up to play a veritable jukebox of selections: the crowd laughed at a drunkard who was trying (with commendable ambition) to tap dance to 'Guantanamera'. It was early morning by the time we cruised back in the Oldsmobile: the streets were deserted, the angel on the Paseo de Reforma lit up eerily in the distance past the statue to Cuauhtémoc.

I reluctantly left Mina at her flat with a feeling that all this talk of virginity needed to be put to the test and that I should try and stay the night with her; but it seemed a mistake to get into a more serious relationship when I was leaving the DF for good the next day, and it had been such a wonderful evening that I didn't want to spoil it with some blundering, stupid move. So I said goodbye. And felt light-headed as I did my last circumnavigation of the *Periférico* Ring Road back to my bed.

Cuernavaca and the South

When the sun came up that same morning I hit the road for Cuernavaca. Once out of the smog and traffic of Mexico City, the roads emptied and I could put my foot down and give the Oldsmobile some much needed exercise.

A red sports car drove up on the inside lane beside me and flashed its lights as it revved. Inside were four guys in leather jackets. Like mine, their car had no numberplates. They seemed to want a race and I was ready for one.

I floored the throttle and the Oldsmobile simply took off, with their car in hot pursuit. It took them a while to catch up. The Oldsmobile in full cry was a magnificent beast.

Their driver was a maniac. He started hooting and flashing his lights at me even more. I laughed. Then he tried to overtake me on the inside and cut me up. It was all getting a little serious. I pulled over to show they had won.

Next minute all four of them were surrounding the car with guns in my face.

'Get out of the car.'

It was a bad moment. When they told me they were police, I wasn't sure if things had got better or worse.

'Why didn't you pull over straight away, *pendejo*, you stupid bastard?

I pleaded ignorance in my worst Spanish. They searched the car. It was lucky I had refused Ramón's offer of a packet of dope as a goodbye present. And I proudly showed them both my Mexican driving licence and my British passport.

'Fucking Ster-leen Moss,' said the driver.

They swaggered back to their car, buckling the guns up, and went off in their leather jackets.

It was the start of a strange day.

When I arrived at the golf club, I found the forty or so permanent staff waiting outside as a reception committee. The maître d' of the restaurant stepped forward as their spokesperson with a short welcoming speech. The gist of it was 'could they all keep their old jobs, please?'

I felt like a man who had unexpectedly inherited a title and country house, with attached rolling acres of land – or rather an eighteen-hole golf course in a prime bit of Cuernavaca, Mexico's most expensive city.

There was a lush fairway, with a riot of tropical flowers and ornamental lakes, and peacocks wandering freely over the grounds. The golf course had been built by General Plutarco Elías Calles in the Twenties. Calles had taken the Mexican Revolution and 'institutionalised' it into what became the PRI, the *Partido Revolucionario Institucional*, the Orwellian-sounding Institutional Revolutionary Party, which had been running the country ever since.

One of the most corrupt of all Mexican presidents in a competitive market, Calles had come here to entertain his cronies for long drunken weekends. And as befitted a man who had started his career in the north as a Pancho Villa-style bandit, although without his charisma, they were very drunken weekends indeed. A special committee room was built so he could hold cabinet meetings when they were too incapacitated to make it back to Mexico City. It was still a place of considerable comfort, both for the visiting golfers and for the club's newest and only resident guest, myself.

During the financial interregnum, all other guests were barred. I moved into the best room in the house, the one Calles himself had used. There was a library, a private swimming pool and a remarkably fine cellar. In the mornings I could fish for breakfast in the private lake. The biggest choice I had to make each day was how I wanted my steak done.

I should have had the time of my life. But as in all the best paradises, the serpent was also present – in this case, in my gut. The amoebal dysentery that had been lurking in wait for me ever since I got to Mexico had finally arrived. The odd symptom had troubled me before but I had been able to ignore it. Now it was here big time. I suspected it was the lettuce I'd had with some *enchiladas suizas* on that final evening with Mina in Mexico City.

Not many of the steaks stayed in my system for long. I blessed the fact that I had a bathroom big enough for Calles to have held cabinet meetings in, a huge Twenties affair of marble and porcelain. It was a place where I spent many intimate moments.

True amoebal dysentery is a bulimic experience: the appetite seems to quicken with each purging. Try as I might to restrain myself and keep to Ritz biscuits and soup, the lure of a rich and free menu kept pulling me back – Gregorio would offer up an

intoxicating but nauseous mixture of steak, salmon and champagne, rather as Montezuma had fed Cortés on turkey, dog, chocolate and chilli.

Gregorio, or 'Gollo', was the maître d' who had headed up the
reception committee. He had started off his career as a barman
and insisted on mixing my drinks for me every evening. Then he
ceremoniously presented me with the menu. As I knew the menu
off by heart before the second week and was the only guest, this
formality was gratuitous, but gave him great pleasure.

He knew all about Tequila Oils. His theory was that I should
just keep drinking ever stronger ones to 'help kill the *amoebitas*'.
Gollo was from central casting: balding, melancholic and with
breath smelling of metal and cloves, he was imperturbable enough
to offer up a Crème de Menthe with tomato juice if asked by one
of the golfing wives who were the main patrons of the place during
the day.

An American doctor (Cuernavaca was full of failed American
doctors) prescribed some antibiotics, which did nothing. Only
later did I learn from a Swiss tourist that the only way to beat
dysentery was to have a faeces sample analysed by a laboratory
and get exactly the right antibiotic for your particular strain of
dysentery: 'Otherwise the amoebas will eat the penicillin for
breakfast.'

I wandered around Cuernavaca on a cocktail of antibiotics,
the club's champagne and a natural light-headedness brought
on by the dysentery. It was an odd city anyway, a city built as
an escape. Since the time of the Aztecs, it had been a natural
retreat down over the mountains from the centre of things in
Mexico City. The bougainvillea, poinsettias and acacia were at
their most rampant in the decaying Borda pleasure gardens,
which the ill-fated Emperor Maximilian and Carlotta used to

visit; even more evocative for me was Cortés's own palace by the main square.

Cortés had built it after his conquest of the country, to share with his new wife, the aristocratic daughter of a Spanish count. The building had a Moorish feel to it, which did not surprise me. Cortés, as befitted a Spaniard of his generation, was obsessed by the Moors, not just as the natural enemy, but as a source of endless romantic legend.

He and his *conquistadores* had arrived in the New World with the *Amadis de Gaul* in their baggage. The *Amadis de Gaul* was the type of romance satirised so ably by Cervantes in *Don Quixote*, a saga in which single knights defeated thousands of the perfidious enemy and still got the girl at the end. Cortés, or Don Cortés as he now styled himself, liked to think of his knights as perpetuating this age of chivalry.

Cortés was as romantic as any of his followers. Indeed one could argue that without such literary precedents as the *Amadis de Gaul*, he would never have thought up the militarily suicidal plan of invading the huge Aztec empire with a few hundred men, destroying his own boats and marching on the biggest city in the world. It was a graphic illustration of the power of imaginative literature, in the same way that man might never have wanted to get to the moon if it had not been for science fiction.

As the nineteenth-century historian Prescott put it in my battered old copy of *The Conquest of Mexico:*

He was a knight-errant in the literal sense of the word. Of all the band of adventurous cavaliers whom Spain, in the sixteenth century, sent forth on the career of discovery and conquest, there was none more deeply filled with the spirit of romantic enterprise that Hernando Cortés. Dangers and difficulties, instead of deterring, seemed to have a charm in his eyes. They were necessary to rouse him to a full consciousness of his powers.

One can see this in the elaborate letters that Cortés despatched to his emperor back in Spain, Charles V, which are full of the Old World language of the romances, even when describing actions that were brutal and expedient:

> We were amazed to see with what fury and dash they suddenly came on. Six horsemen and myself who were nearer than the others charged forward into the midst of them. They, frightened of the horses, began to fly, and so we spurred out of the city after them, killing many, although in grave danger ourselves. ('The siege of Xochimilco', *Third Letter to the Emperor Charles V*)

Once the actual conquest was over, Cortés suffered a sad decline. Having married a prime piece of Spanish aristocracy, one might have thought that the newly ennobled Marqués would have rested on his laurels and cultivated the vineyards he planted in Cuernavaca to go with the palace. Certainly Charles V encouraged him to do just that, rewarding him with large tracts of land and money, yet keeping the crown's political power vested in the separate and supposedly more dispassionate hands of a series of temporary viceroys.

Rather than settling down, Cortés was always restless. He embarked on a series of ever more foolhardy projects: some fruitless voyages up to the Gulf of California in search of mythical cities of gold, voyages that ended in shipwreck and the loss of a large part of his fortune; the Mexicans still call the Gulf the 'Sea of Cortés', while it is thought Cortés named California itself after a heroine called Queen Califia in one of the romances he had read; there were also punitive further journeys down south through what became the Banana Republics of Guatemala and Honduras, during which he came close to losing it completely when stuck in yet another jungle and faced by mutiny, mosquitoes and disease. He rounded on the hapless Cuauhtémoc, whom he had brought along as a hostage to ensure the Aztecs didn't rise up behind him. Cortés accused the deposed emperor of conspiracy and executed him. This last unnecessary act came to play on his conscience later more than the subjection of a whole people, perhaps because it was so clearly unchivalric.

Faced by mounting debts, Cortés went back to Spain to plead with the emperor for more money. This was a mistake. He was kept waiting forever in the ante-rooms of the Hapsburg Empire. In a bizarre fulfilment of all his early fantasies, he ended up fighting the Moors at the siege of Algiers and was outraged when the rest of the Spaniards abandoned their attack. To make matters worse, he and his son were shipwrecked and lost the most precious of the surviving Aztec crown jewels.

Worn out by litigation, he died while still in Spain, his reputation eclipsed by the yet greater riches that his far more brutal follower Pizarro had since achieved in Peru. So there was never much time to enjoy the palace in Cuernavaca.

The palace had been allowed to decay over the centuries. By the time Prescott wrote his history, in 1843, it was not much more than 'a half-ruined barrack, although a most picturesque object, standing on a hill, behind which starts up the great white volcano'. It had now been restored as a government building, but there was little favourable about Cortés to be found inside. Instead Diego Rivera, the prolific artist of the Revolution and Mr Frida Kahlo, had painted vivid murals over the palace wall of Indians being branded by the conquistadors.

There were several agreeable cafés around the square from which I could contemplate Cortés's palace and reflect on my hero's sad fall into historical limbo, as with true bulimic courage I munched on the German *küchen* and patisseries which to my surprise were common in Cuernavaca. It turned out that there were many retired Germans as well as Americans wandering around in checked shirts and ill-advised shorts. In truth the whole place was one giant retirement home. The agreeable altitude and climate, together with Cuernavaca's billing as the 'city of eternal spring', meant that there were more Decembers than Mays promenading its restful streets.

Plenty of American writers had been drawn here by the combination of low rents and the desire to be 'South of Boston south of Washington, / south of any bearing', as Robert Lowell put it when he came in the late 1960s – a rare bit of travelling by a writer who never usually left the confines of his own head. He was following in the footsteps of the poet Hart Crane, who had proclaimed of Mexico, 'Here I feel that life is real; people really live and die here. In Paris they were just cutting paper dollies.'

Lowell was fifty when he arrived in Cuernavaca at midwinter and promptly fell in love with a girl of 'some sweet uncertain age, say twenty-seven', whom he 'kissed so much you thought you were walked on'; together they attempted to climb 'the Volcano [no need for Lowell to explain which one – its readers were expected to pick up on the allusion to Popocatépetl], when we charged so far beyond our courage-altitude . . .'

The affair petered out in the 'high fever' of Mexico, but not before Lowell had come up with one of the most candid of male reflections on an affair: 'Did anyone ever sleep with anyone / without thinking a split second he was God?'

One reason why Lowell's readers were supposed to pick up on

the reference to 'the Volcano' was because Malcolm Lowry had already made it the literary volcano of all time in his masterpiece, *Under the Volcano*: a novel accurately described in the ISBN listing of the copy I had with me as 'Alcoholism – Mexico – Psychology – Fiction'.

Lowry's presence still brooded over the city. Set in 1938, around the time both Graham Greene and Evelyn Waugh were writing their own Mexican tales, *Under the Volcano* was an account of Geoffrey Firmin's last day as Honorary British Consul in Cuernavaca, a day that happened also to be the Day of the Dead in Mexico – All Saints' Day.

Although driven by the collapse of Geoffrey Firmin's marriage and body, largely due to alcohol, it contained a detailed description of both Cuernavaca (the golf club was mentioned on the very first page of the novel) and of the Mexican psyche, perhaps more carefully and intuitively than either Greene or Waugh. For a start Lowry spoke the language – and had stayed for more than a token visit (Greene spent only five weeks in the country). The rituals of drinking he described were those I recognised: one man toasted his friend for continued *salud y pesetas*, 'health and money'; the other replied, '*Y tiempo para gastarlas*, and time to enjoy them in.'

The actual drinking was prodigious. The Consul had a jerry-built pulley system made out of a towel so that his first drink of the day could be winched up to him if his hand was shaking too much. This was the same system the author used himself. Anyone trying the trick students played with *Withnail and I*, when they match the drinking in the film glass for glass, would never make it through *Under the Volcano*.

With his soon-to-be ex-wife Jan Gabrial, Lowry had lived in a side street called the Calle Humboldt; when I went to look for it, book in hand, no one was too sure which was his house, or even if it had survived at all, as the street was constantly being both rebuilt and renumbered – an apt memorial for his novel of disintegration.

Lowry did, however, seem to have time to work on his handicap while in Cuernavaca, although I felt I was the only reader of *Under the Volcano* to be looking for the golfing references; the Consul comes across some of his old golf balls when hiding a bottle of whisky and is reminded that he 'can still carry the eighth green in three'. As a fifteen-year-old back in England, Lowry had won a junior golf championship and nursed ambitions to be a pro. I could imagine him propping up the mahogany of the clubhouse bar here.

No previous critics had ever explored the interesting possibility that Lowry and the Consul's mutual alcoholism was not due to the failure of their marriages or to fatalism induced by Mexico; Lowry drank because he had never made the grade as a professional golfer. It was really like an American sporting story: the college jock who has gone to seed.

Meanwhile my own duties back at the club were, to say the least, light. I had my own electric caddy with which I toured the grounds, although it wasn't powerful enough to have much fun. Antonio, the club trainer, gave me the odd coaching session, but the attractions of trying to get a small white ball into a hole a long way away were beyond me; most evenings I stayed up late playing backgammon with Gollo over the club's wine.

I asked Gollo once if he remembered an English writer and golf player with a good handicap who had lived in Cuernavaca just before the war and drank a lot. Gollo was old enough to have been working there then. He just shrugged: '¿*Quién sabe*? Who knows? All the English who come here drink a lot.' I didn't take it personally.

Meanwhile I took care that anything Gollo and I drank ourselves was left out of the inventory I had been charged by the bank to complete. To help me compile this list of the club's possessions, I had the enthusiastic services of one Leopoldo, an athletic boy of about my age. We went through the club from top to bottom, counting every leather-tooled book, elephant-foot club-holder and silver spoon. I would call out the item and Leopoldo would note it down in a ledger with the retentive and bureaucratic instinct of every Mexican.

I began to have fun with the inventory:

Item: two ashtrays of nubile women, silver, possibly silver-plated, standing on bullet-shell casings, women sculpted in the *churriguresque* style;
Item: portrait of young Indian servant in headdress, looking distinctly like Johnny Rotten.

Leopoldo was puzzled. 'Do you mean Joseph Cotten?' He was better on films than music.

In the attic rooms we found trunks of papers with Elías Calles's initials. We lifted the lid on one to find stacks of lottery coupons inside. A scorpion scuttled over my hand when I opened the next, deterring my quest for any further historical investigation.

'Just put "Item: Trunks of antiquities, various",' I told Leopoldo.

I left the inventory of the cellar until the last day so we could keep drinking it. Apart from the champagne, which was French and the real thing, as Gollo kept assuring me, it was a hit and miss collection of Mexican reds from private estates, many unlabelled, which ranged, so my tasting notes tell me, from the rich and profound to some so tannic you could pickle chillies in them. When Leopoldo and I had inspected the last dusty bottle and locked them away as now untouchable, I invited him out for a meal to celebrate.

We stopped off at Leopoldo's shack of a home for him to change. I caught a glimpse of an achingly beautiful wife, who must have been all of sixteen and was shy. Leopoldo was refreshingly upfront about their married life – they were expecting a child but he was also seeing several other women.

Later, at one of Cuernavaca's many *cantinas* (Lowry had counted fifty-seven), Leopoldo expanded even more over a few drinks: he told me that the local police force were well known for killing guys they didn't like and then covering it up. His own brother-in-law had been killed by the police for not paying enough alimony; this last story seemed complicated and unlikely enough to be true.

It was hardly surprising that Leopoldo was expansive. For we were not drinking the usual tequila. When I'd asked for one, the barman had spat on the sawdust floor, alarmingly close to my feet: '¿*Tequila*? ¡*Para maricones*! ¡*Y Mariachis*! Tequila is just for pussies. And mariachi players. Here we drink mezcal. *Puro mezcal de Oaxaca*. Pure Oaxaca mezcal.'

He produced a bottle that far from being pure looked cloudy, but not so cloudy that I could miss the large worm floating at the bottom. Nor was it the tourist type of worm they put in a novelty bottle either, but a fleshy, decomposing, honest-to-god cactus-fed worm. I surrendered and asked for a glass of the stuff. 'We don't sell it *por el vaso*, by the glass,' said the barman in disgust. '*Es por botella*, it's by the bottle.' He slammed one down on the table.

I was well aware of Lowry's views on mezcal, which he enjoyed for its close but false association with mescaline (so spelling it 'mescal') and for its cheapness: in his novel, the Consul calculated with a drinker's logic that '900 pesos = 100 bottles of whisky =

900 bottles of tequila. Argal [Ergo]: one should drink neither tequila nor whisky but mescal.' No wonder he kept getting hallucinations. One of Lowry's poems was entitled 'Thirty-five Mescals in Cuautla'. I couldn't match that, nor wanted to.

Even so, by the time I got back to the club I was roaring. Mezcal is one of those drinks that grabs you by the throat and refuses to let go – insistent, declamatory and intoxicating in a way that not all alcoholic drinks necessarily are. I had what seemed the brilliant idea of taking out the caddy and doing a moonlit drive around the grounds. To my disappointment, even at full throttle the caddy made it around the course without careering into any bunker or other absurd golf feature. I abandoned it by the swimming pool and stumbled across a peacock, which raised its feathered crown against the light of the moon.

Next day on waking, I took a final photo of myself with my caribou cowboy boots up on Calles's desk, as if I were Pancho Villa or Zapata invading his palace, then I had a last breakfast of *huevos rancheros* and said farewell to Gollo, Leopoldo and the rest. I felt bad because I knew the bank planned to turn the club into an American-style leisure centre, complete with pinball and exercise classes. I just hoped it didn't come to anything (most of the bank's plans didn't).

Julio told me on the phone that there had been an upset when our overall boss visited the bank's branch in Guatemala. The branch manager had walked outside with the boss and been shot dead in front of him by a man who claimed title to his *finca*, 'ranch'. Julio was shocked: 'I just can't believe the way they do business in Guatemala.'

The Oldsmobile had been lovingly polished by the club's mechanic. Even the ashtray had been cleaned out. I hit the road feeling good about myself and with some cash wired from Julio in my pocket. My previous evening's drinking had indeed finally killed off the last of the amoebas, as Gollo had predicted, and I was now blissfully dry-bowelled.

It was time for the final drive on to the South.

*

In Cuernavaca, I had been within distant sight of my old adversary Popocatépetl. Now I was even more under the volcano as I skirted around its southern side to get to Veracruz: it reared over the small town of Cholula.

The pyramid in Cholula was so big that I missed it. The main road through the town ran past the bottom of what looked like a scruffy hill. Only the next morning did I realise that it was one of the most ancient and sacred of Mexican sites.

This was where Cortés had won the soul of the country before even defeating the Aztecs in battle. Prescott had a terrific passage about how he had stood on top of the pyramid, a central religious site for the whole of Ancient Mexico, and vowed to build a church for every day of the year. As a result churches covered the city. There was even an ungainly church on top of the grassed-over pyramid.

Cholula had been the centre for the cult of Quetzalcoatl, the most peaceable of all the pre-Columbian gods. Legend had it that he had left the Toltecs (and so by definition their descendants, the Aztecs) because of a ruckus in the God World and had gone 'across the sea' to return on an appointed day in the future. It was a legend that Cortés was lucky to exploit when he arrived on the very calendrical day that Quetzalcoatl would have come back across the same sea. There was a certain irony (and truth) in this iden-tification, in that Quetzalcoatl was the one god who was thought to disapprove of human sacrifice. Tlacaelel had banished him from the pantheon of gods in Tenochtitlán as being insufficiently bellicose. However, in Cholula his temple and cult continued up to Cortés's arrival, as a rival theology to the bloodthirsty Aztec one.

I had a wonderful moment outside one of the little churches whose every last crevice was ornately decorated with bright Mexican tiles and carvings. It was early evening and 'Popo' (as the Mexicans, when feeling friendly towards the mountain, liked to call it) had taken on even more of a Japanese look than ever, with a thin wisp of smoke coming out. The bells were pealing, there was the excited laughter of unseen children coming from somewhere near by and the smell of roasting chocolate and peanuts from one of the little roadside stalls. A band were playing at the next church down the way – all the churches were very close together – and the sound carried in the evening air with the clarity of a cinema soundtrack. I had what I can only describe as an epiphany, a moment of lucid and complete surrender, in which the whole of Mexico seemed to come up inside me and I felt that this was a moment that would never end and that wherever I went I would not leave this place.

As Billie Holiday sang, 'you got it bad, and that ain't good'.

*

I was coming down out of the mountains to the Gulf of Mexico, the first time I had seen the south-eastern coast. There were women selling bunches of the large white Mexican lilies on the side of the road; I bought some and they filled the Oldsmobile with their heavy incense.

Veracruz lay ahead, the town of the 'true cross' as Cortés named it when he first landed there, by all accounts the funkiest city in

Mexico, and the reports were not misleading. Even Paul Theroux, that most misanthropic of travellers, who had passed through Mexico with his hand to his nose and a general disdain for the dirt and the noise, had ended up liking Veracruz at least a little.

There were non-stop mariachis in the square, seafood *a la veracruzana*, in a tomato, pepper and chilli sauce, and the constant bustle of a city that was both an active port and a pleasure destination for day-trippers from the mountains. They even sold whelks (or what looked like a close relation).

The bars on the square were overpriced tourist traps, so I went off down the backstreets towards the port, where there were plenty of plain *cantinas*. They were lit by a single bare 60-watt bulb in the centre of the room, so that framed in the window, or through the cheap plastic strips of colour that hung down on the doors, you could see the tableaux of Mexican drinking life from afar: the plain table, the old cardboard boxes of beer bottles and soft drinks in a corner and usually one talker holding the floor to an audience either indifferent or comatose.

I hadn't been on a serious drinking jag for a while and this was the place to cut loose. I found myself at two in the morning in an insalubrious *cantina* with some Colombian sailors. The *cantina* had one feature unusual even for Veracruz: the serving bar was also the urinal, so that you could relieve yourself without having to leave your drink. At the end of the evening, the Colombians offered me a passage back home with them in their boat to Cartagena, but I wasn't that drunk.

By some miracle I didn't even have a hangover the next day. Veracruz was that kind of a place. I went for a spin along the promenade lined by pink railings. When I stopped to let someone pull out of a parking space, a Volkswagen Beetle went straight into the back of the Oldsmobile with a noise like a collapsing balloon.

I got out, calmly under the circumstances (I was after all getting used to this), to inspect the damage; there was none. The Oldsmobile was so heavy that while the front bonnet of the Beetle had folded up like a tin can, I had come off without a scratch. I even smiled at the guy. Nothing was going to ruin my day.

Mocambo Beach was just out of town and a fly-blown affair compared to the fabulous beaches of the Pacific I had been to: the sand was gritty and floating on the water there were traces of oil (most of Mexico's came from the Gulf). I ate tamarind ice cream and watched a family of Mexicans struggle with their heavy, old-fashioned bathing costumes as they changed behind towels. One of the girls had beautiful breasts. Suddenly I felt very English again.

I wasn't hanging around now. As I set off down the Gulf for Tabasco and Villahermosa, the radio had a melodramatic message about electric storms up ahead. The horizon was as flat and peaceful as the rim of a toilet.

I had Graham Parker playing on the tape-deck: 'Passion is no ordinary word ... Everything's a thrill and every girl's a kill. And then it gets unreal, and then you don't feel anything ...'

I thought of all those writers who had come to Mexico in search of the different and ended up disliking the place: from the dyspeptic Paul Theroux, whose *The Old Patagonian Express* had just come out (even first-class railway travel in Mexico, he complained, was 'both uncomfortable and dirty'), to the 1930s British generation of D. H. Lawrence, Evelyn Waugh, Aldous Huxley and Graham Greene ('how I loathed Mexico ...'). It can't have helped that none of them spoke more than a few words of Spanish.

A remarkable and little commented upon phenomenon was that so many of the finest English writers of the inter-war years should have gravitated towards Mexico, hardly a natural choice, either geographically or culturally. Moreover Greene, Huxley and Lawrence all produced both a travel book and a novel from their visit. This was only partly to defray costs – 'Hey I'm in the country already, let's get two books out of the deal'; perhaps they did not find the real Mexico on their travels to be quite what they expected, so had to fictionalise it instead.

Graham Greene exemplified this. *The Lawless Roads* was a miserable travel book, one steeped in loathing for both the country and himself. At one point he talked of his 'pathological hatred' for the country. Yet *The Power and the Glory* was considered one of his finest novels: a conflict between the priesthood and the State concentrated in the character of a nameless 'whisky priest' who is persecuted in Tabasco and Villahermosa under the anti-clerical laws enacted by my golf-playing buddy, President Calles.

Greene had hoped to see more of this dramatic conflict for himself. For years he had fantasised about Mexico before going there in 1939. But he never got close enough to the action, or for that matter spent enough time trying to do so. All that Greene was left with after his actual short journey of five weeks through the country were ticks in his buttocks; he had ridden an infested mule through the area I was now crossing in the Oldsmobile.

Perhaps the disappointment felt by those writers of the Thirties about Mexico was because they all, with the exception of Evelyn Waugh, assumed the old Romantic idea that travel was a form of liberal and cultural education. Waugh's attitude was more contemporary – that one travelled, above all, 'to escape boredom'. He went to Mexico 'to verify and reconsider impressions formed at a distance', and was honest about the disparity between such preconceptions and the reality of what he found:

The truthful travel book rarely works to a climax; the climax is sometimes the moment of disembarkation and everything beyond it an attempt to revive artificially, under the iron lung of rhythmic, day to day observation, the revelation of first acquaintance.

Waugh had been the most perceptive as well about what writers looked for in Mexico, particularly those, like him, who were already seasoned travellers:

> . . . one needs to go to the moon, or some such place, to recapture the excitement with which one first landed at Calais. For many people Mexico has, in the past, had this lunar character. Lunar it still remains, but in no poetic sense. It is waste land, part of a dead or, at any rate, a dying planet.

As I drove on with the Oldsmobile's insulated air-conditioning purring beneath me, I began to think that travel was like an extended arcade game: scenery moving through and past the windscreen in wraparound colour, my music of choice on the tape-deck and with the occasional pit-stop at garages or motels. Far from being a stimulus to thought, travel was a sedative, a form of ambient video entertainment flowing ceaselessly past you in a non-stop stream of landscapes and other peoples' lives that could distract you from your own.

Unfortunately as with all good sedatives, like Valium, it came with a depressive kickback and in my case I could feel the foot looming up to kick as I got nearer to the border and Belize. Selling the car was no longer a theoretical end to the journey; it was an imminent and practical necessity about which I still knew not much more than the man in the plane had told me. In all my journeys through Mexico, I had met no one else who thought that it was an advisable or practical proposition.

But I was getting closer to the ruins of Palenque. I had wanted desperately to see some of the Maya sites – one justification for having the car, as some could only be reached by road – and Palenque lay not far off my route. The rains came on as I approached, and I peered out at the jungle shrub surrounding Palenque through a windscreen that even the Oldsmobile's powerful wipers had trouble keeping clean. I discovered that, according to the locals, it was always raining here; indeed that each of the neighbouring villages laid claim to being the wettest place in the country, just as they do in some parts of Wales and Cumbria.

There was a cut-price hostel in the village of Palenque, some way from the ruins, where I slept on cheap nylon sheets that slid with the dampness of the place, as I twisted and turned to avoid the various biting insects. A German traveller at the hotel quoted me a line he said was Goethe's over breakfast: that anyone who thought the small nuisances of life were bearable had never spent the night in a room with a mosquito.

The ruins more than made up for it. The main buildings were raised on small mounds that had been cleared; there was a penumbra of nearby buildings that were only partially cleared and then, supposedly, many more distant ones in the circumference that had not.

The Maya architecture of Palenque, while often just as big as the Aztec I had seen before, was also more intimate, decorative and peaceful. The analogy often used was that the Maya, whose long-lived civilisation had survived in different parts of Central America from at least 500 BC, were like the Greeks, with their city-states, their learning and their supposedly more rational and peaceful ways; the Aztecs, whose brilliant and aggressive decline and fall was compressed into a few centuries before the Spanish Conquest, were more like the Romans.

The physiognomy of the Maya helped this comparison: the classic large, hooked nose profile I saw everywhere in Palenque, whether on the portraits depicted on the temple walls or on their descendants who filled my car or sold me bread, seemed benign and contemplative. Yet if there was an analogy with any of the cultures of the Old World, it was perhaps with the Arabic rather than the Greek – the endlessly interwoven decorative motifs of the roof-combs and the creation of intimate spaces among the monumental.

I climbed up the main Temple of the Inscriptions, or 'El Palacio' as John Lloyd Stephens described it in his vivid account of first coming here in 1839, which he gave the prosaic title *Incidents of Travel in Central America, Chiapas and Yucatan*. Stephens, like his fellow American Prescott, author of the *History of the Conquest of Mexico*, and the explorer Humboldt, were part of a wave of interest in Latin America that grew in the first half of the nineteenth century and which lifted the curtain on the continent after the long dusty centuries of Spanish rule came to an end.

Stephens wrote with a matter-of-fact vigour and enthusiasm that was refreshing after the more wearied tones of twentieth-century travellers. When he arrived at Palenque with his friend Frederick Catherwood, a British engraver, after a terrible journey negotiating the rains and the politics of Central America, they let off '*a feu-de-joie* of four rounds each, being the last charge of our firearms'. This was, as Stephens engagingly points out, as much to warn the locals of their powers of self-defence as out of exuberance. But it was his account of their first night at the ruins, when they slept in the Palacio itself, which was so compelling:

The rain continued, with heavy thunder and lightning, all the afternoon. In the absolute necessity of taking up our abode among the ruins, we had hardly thought of our exposure to the elements until it was forced upon us. At night we could not light a candle, but the darkness of the place was lit up by fireflies of extraordinary size and brilliance, shooting through the corridors and stationary on the walls, forming a beautiful and striking spectacle.

What they had first seen lit up by the fireflies, and what Catherwood was then to capture in drawings that remain the epitome of the 'romance of lost civilisation', were some of the most beautiful Maya inscriptions and temples that have survived.

Climbing up the Palacio, I was prepared for the Hollywood trick the Maya had constructed ahead: a secret staircase that led from the top of the pyramid back down inside it to the burial chamber of a ruler. The secret staircase – it was difficult to use any other less melodramatic term – had only been discovered in 1949, long after Stephens and Catherwood, when an archaeologist noticed holes filled with stone plugs in one of the floor slabs; the temple wall also extended below ground level, suggesting some lower chamber. When they lifted the slab, they found a stairway so densely filled with rubble that it took three years to get to the bottom.

Going down the corbelled staircase on my own felt like something out of John Buchan. Visitors were asked to bring their own torches, as there was only a set of low-voltage lights running from an intermittent generator.

For the archaeologists who first saw the funeral vault at the bottom, it must have been the revelation of a lifetime: the room was still preserved as they had found it, with the large funeral tomb of a king dominating the chamber. The size of the crypt was impressive – it was at least twenty feet high. After the descent down a narrow staircase, this was like finding a cavern after potholing.

The crypt walls were lined with the stucco reliefs of deities. Under the slab, they had found the ruler's skeleton, covered in jade ornaments and with a jade death mask that, to my eyes, looked disconcertingly like Laurence Olivier. The chronological glyphs both here and elsewhere in Palenque revealed some of this ruler's history: he was called Pacal, meaning 'shield', and lived from 603–683 during the period of the city-state's greatest prosperity. As king, Pacal would have been expected to take part in the ritual celebrations that attended feast days, including the use of inebriating enemas, which seemed beyond the call of duty.

When his subjects buried him, they left six young men as attendants to wait at the bottom of the stairs outside and backfilled the staircase with rubble; to ensure that Pacal's spirit could still watch over them, a stone snake ran from the grave up the stairs to the entrance above.

Going down to the tomb had thrown me a little, particularly as there were no other travellers around. It was past midday, so I came out from the funeral vaults to the full heat of the sun. I headed off down a path behind the Temple of the Lion, a crumbling building that had been lived in for a year or two by the eccentric Count Walbech, again in the early part of the nineteenth century. He was an adventurer who helped popularise the theory that the Maya must have been influenced by 'us' (they couldn't have done it all themselves could they?); he postulated various theories to show that just about everyone from the Hindus to the Egyptians had sailed the Atlantic to help them. Diffusionists had been promoting the same cause ever since.

The path off into the surrounding rainforest was a scrappy one that started broad and imperceptibly narrowed as you went along, as if people taking it before had started to turn back. It went past one of the many small streams that surrounded the site and I stopped and splashed around in a pool. I had no food with me, on the false assumption that there would be some to buy at the ruins.

Light-headed from the sun and lack of lunch, I went further into the forest down one of the branching trails, aimlessly looking for some of the more deserted temples. I had been fascinated by one particular engraving of Palenque by Catherwood: it showed an old, overgrown temple, with trees coming through the stone-work both of the steps and of the temple roof itself, and liana-like tendrils curling around the tree trunks. I couldn't find it. The temple had probably either rotted into debris or been immaculately restored – either way it was likely to be unrecognisable.

Two things happened: at around four o'clock, as so often, it started to rain, and when I tried to head back, I realised I had got lost.

It was an absurd feeling. I was hardly in the middle of the jungle. Yet because Palenque was not in a very populated area, if I kept heading in the wrong direction I soon would be. As in the best fairy tales, it had started to get dark. The jungle seemed to present a sort of dull muddy-green in every direction. The heavy rain falling from the leaves sounded like the padding of a jaguar. I felt like Mole in the Wild Wood. I was also getting very wet.

After an hour or so of stumbling around in ever decreasing circles and getting nowhere, I sheltered under a tree. A man came by with a child on his back. '¿*Ruinas*?' I shouted at him, pointlessly (where else would I want to go?) He looked at me strangely and gave me directions with an arm that wavered only a fraction.

It took a while to get back and was dark by the time I reached the ruins; they were officially shut. The night watchman, the '*velador*', had to unlock the chain over the gate to let me out, with much grumbling about 'hippies' (there was a group of them who hung out at a trailer park in the village and were unpopular with the locals).

Being called a hippy was the last insult I needed. I was already soaked to the skin.

*

Next day I woke up feeling feverish. The brackish coffee in the pension didn't help. There was a simple choice: stay in Palenque and rest up or drive it out of my system. I decided to drive.

I was starting to come up into the Yucatan peninsula proper. Cortés had famously crushed a piece of paper in his hand when asked by his emperor to describe the physical shape of Mexico – a story I liked not only because he was right, but because it revealed so much of the man's character, the *coup de théâtre* of the showman playing to the gallery. But if most of Mexico was mountainous, the Yucatan was as flat as East Anglia on a wet afternoon.

Cortés never penetrated the Yucatan, though he passed the peninsula by boat on the way to Veracruz. The little contact he did have with its people may well have discouraged him: the Maya greeted the conquistadors as rapacious invaders who must be defeated at all costs; unlike the Aztecs, they did not think of them as returning gods. It was not until much later that the Spaniards were able to conquer them. The Yucatan was another country, by geography, by race and even, I thought, by temperament. Only a historical accident had prevented it from becoming a separate Central American state.

It was the first time I had ever been bored driving the Oldsmobile. The long roads into the peninsula stretched away in monotonous straight lines, with a flat horizon of forest ahead.

Seeing an aeroplane in the distance was an event, as was stopping for petrol. There were not even any hitch-hikers.

I filled up in Escárcega where the road divided: the main road carried up into the northern Yucatan and the other great cities of the Maya like Uxmal and Chichén Itzá; it also led to the fabulous resort town of Cancún on the coast, a place that some decried as vulgarity itself but which I liked the sound of – a Las Vegas on the Caribbean, as if 'the strip' had been built along a sandbar. The smaller road less travelled by, which I needed to take, cut across the peninsula to Chetumal and the border with Belize. It also passed some remote, little-visited Maya ruins.

The guy at the petrol station filled me up for the long trip across the jungle. I was feeling so lonely that it was good to chat with him. I asked how far it was to Chetumal. He shrugged and unrolled the carpet ahead of him. I hadn't seen that gesture since Texas and laughed.

A couple of miles down the road I looked at the petrol gauge: it was still showing empty. This time I didn't laugh. The bastard had pulled the oldest trick in the book: he had left the previous guy's total up on the gauge, pretended to fill me up and then charged for an empty tank.

I stormed back. He was, of course, waiting for me.

'OK, let's have a full tank this time – I've already paid for it.'

'No you haven't.'

He looked at me, impassive. The owner came out of his shack, a middle-aged man with a light straw hat perched on a Robert Morley face. 'You heard him – do you want petrol again, or not?'

There wasn't another petrol station for fifty miles. I had no choice. The owner insisted on holding on to the car keys until I had paid.

I felt wired up and lonelier still as I drove across the plateau. It was a completely deserted road: I passed no other cars, or for that matter any people. I tried playing the most soulful music I had, Van Morrison and Graham Parker, but still felt despondent.

There were some small Maya sites along the way that no one visited because they were way down on the archaeological league: Becán, Chicanna and Xpuhil were overgrown and wild, with nothing to prepare you for a jaguar's head entrance coming at you around a corner or tall, thin towers with trees curling around them. They had the playful, baroque architecture of the sites built in the very last stages of Maya civilisation, not long before the Spanish arrived.

Normally I would have loved these places. But I didn't feel normal. I was tired of empty space and all this evidence of an empty past. I was tired of driving. I was tired of ruins. And I had business to attend to.

BELIZE ENDGAME

'I can't let you out of the country without registration documents for the car.'

I had expected this.

'I'm sorry. I mislaid my papers travelling through from *Los Estados Unidos*, the States.' I gave a big shrug. It was funny how much 'bigger' I had started to make all my gestures in order to be understood in Mexico. I felt like an old afternoon-movie star hamming it up. 'And anyway,' I said, reading my cue card, 'is there no other way we can arrange this matter?' I looked him in the eye, as I had learnt was expected if the transaction was to be completed with honour intact on all sides. My last stash of dollar bills was folded inside my Mexican licence ready for him to inspect.

'No,' said the official wearily, 'there is no other way to arrange this matter.' He had a sombre, sallow appearance. He was also very fat.

I looked at him, incredulous. I couldn't believe that I had driven through 6,000 miles of Mexican roads to be blocked at the exit by my first incorruptible Mexican, a human Cerberus. He was not just bargaining either. He hadn't even looked at the colour of my money; this was genuine refusal.

'¡*Qué dice*! What do you mean!' I screamed, sounding histrionic even to myself, 'There is always another way.'

'No. Unless you have the forms, I cannot let you out of the country, *Señor*. There is a US consul in Chetumal. He can arrange the formalities.' He gestured for me to go. It was time to regroup. I headed back into Chetumal, the Mexican town on the border.

Chetumal was a brutal modern city, with its buildings laid out in a grid. But I did notice that after the relative racial homogeneity of 'mainland' Mexico, there were black, yellow and lily-white skins all around me.

A Mexican in a bar explained it to me: Chetumal was a duty-free port, so people came over the border from Belize to buy luxury goods. And the people of Belize were the most mixed race in the world: the original Maya Indians had been overrun by the Spanish in the usual way; then the British had colonised the country (hence its old name of British Honduras) and introduced Chinese workers for their big cash crop, mahogany; a ship full of slaves bound for the States had been wrecked on the coral reef and the slaves had decided they would have a better time free in Belize than in the plantations of Georgia. As a result, it was the only Central American country to have a significant black population (this was the Mexican's story – the blacks may have also been brought from Jamaica by British settlers). To round off the racial soup, a group of German Mennonites had come at the turn of the century from their own isolated community of back-to-earthers.

I had seen some unmistakable ones striding around with straw hair and pale, staring eyes.

The bad news was that because they all came to shop and then smuggle the goods back to Belize, it was one of the toughest border posts on the continent. I explained my predicament to the guy in the bar.

'Well maybe you should just wait a few days. After all, this *señor* won't be there every day.'

It was a blindingly obvious suggestion. I started to stake the custom post out. I would drive there daily (it was a little way from the town) and check if the fat controller, as I dubbed him, was at his desk. There were three lines of control, but it would be stupid to try to go through on another, as he would be bound to see me. You couldn't go through at night unless your papers had been pre-signed.

I had arrived on a Wednesday. By the following Sunday, the fat controller still hadn't missed a shift. He seemed to be there all that day as well (what was the point of a Catholic country if people didn't go to church?).

I mooched around Chetumal. It was a pit. The place was like one giant Dixons store – everywhere I went, people were hauling radios and ghetto-blasters out of shops. To prove that they all worked, they were turned up to full volume, whether by the shopkeepers or the proud purchasers. There was a cacophony of badly recorded mariachi music and, even worse, the dregs of Seventies American rock music and disco: Boston, Toto, Grand American Funk all seemed to have been offloaded in bulk at the port for a receptive Chetumal public. I imagined cranes swinging huge bales of Peter Frampton records off the tankers.

The hotel I stayed in had all the character and charm of an air-conditioning unit. There was a sterile restaurant with damp tablecloths and warm beer. Maya food was supposed to be 'rich and tropical', but from the evidence of this place it consisted of putting mashed-up banana in otherwise perfectly respectable tortillas, like a kids' version of Mexican cuisine.

I had a lucky break. One day, passing a dingy notary's business, I went in on the off chance. The owner, a Maya Indian with a nose like a soup plate, couldn't forge American registration papers – but he could do me the Mexican papers I would have been issued with at El Paso if I had brought the car in legitimately,

He got to work. I was, as ever, impressed by the casual professionalism with which Mexicans did things. He typed out a form, photocopied it several times, then covered it with deliberately indecipherable stamps in different colours, as if they had been used too often. He wrote an appropriate date on one of them by hand (my visa had long overrun, so we made it seem like I had only been in the country for a legal length of time). The result looked like something out of a Maya codex; I felt like rolling up the paper and tying it with a red ribbon.

It worked. The fat controller bought into it. I couldn't even tell if he remembered me from the time before.

Within the hour I was out of Chetumal and out of Mexico, across the border and heading down into Belize with the Clash at full volume on the tape to blow away any lingering revisionist running-dog disco music that might have clung to me from the place.

There had still been one problem on the Belize side of the border though. The bastards had stamped my passport 'entered with car' and made it clear there was no way that I could 'exit without car'. But I wasn't going to let a little thing like that worry me.

I was home and dry. Almost.

*

Corozal, the first place I came to in Belize, was much more my sort of town. There were funky little shacks, a harbour with some boats and, best of all, a pool hall with a bar that let out a couple of rooms on the side.

Now that it had got hotter I was drinking more beer than tequila, which anyway had to be imported into Belize and so was too expensive. After a few beers and some lobster and rice (the lobster on the bar menu was cheaper than the chicken), I got talking to Roach.

Roach presided over the bar. He was a Jamaican, in his fifties, with deep-black skin and a grizzled look. He was not a great conversationalist, but I didn't want somebody who could talk – I wanted somebody who could listen.

When I had finished telling him about my long journey, I looked at him expectantly.

'So what do you think – can I sell my car?'

'Uh.'

For a moment I thought he hadn't understood me. My English accent was probably as difficult to understand for him as his patois English was for me.

'My car. Do you think I can sell it here?'

Roach looked at me as if I were stupid. 'Of course. You've come to the right place. Everybody in Belize wants an American car. Might even want it myself. Where is it? Let's take a look.'

There were no other punters in the bar, so he locked up and we went round the side to where I had left it in the shade.

Roach started to laugh – big, sobbing laughs that rocked his considerable frame.

The car was, admittedly, a bit of a mess, but nothing that a bucket of water couldn't put right.

'I'm sorry, but you've made one big mistake. This car only has two doors.'

'So. It's an Oldsmobile 98, prime condition, with electric windows.' I demonstrated. 'It's only supposed to have two doors.'

'Down here, we want four-door cars. There's only one way anybody can afford to have a car, and that's if they use it part-time as a taxi. A two-door car is useless as a taxi, however big it is. And even if anybody wanted your car, they would never sell it on to anybody else. There's no *resale value*.' He stressed *resale value* with relish and looked at me with his pool-ball black eyes.

I rocked back on my heels. 'Holy fuck.' For the first time in my life, I realised the full value and meaning of the term 'market research'.

It was time for some of Roach's imported tequila. I showed him how to mix up a makeshift Tequila Oil. I didn't have much money left, so I thought I might as well be reckless with it.

'What am I going to do?'

'You can ask around town. Try Mr Kluivert over at the hotel. Maybe you'll find something.' He shrugged. It was not his problem.

But my problem was now a very real one. The little remaining money I had would run out within the week. I had been counting on selling the car to get me back to Mexico City and then to England.

That night I hardly slept for the frustration of it all. When I got up early and walked along the shore, I came across an old guy sanding down a dinghy, presumably a tender for one of the yachts bobbing out in the bay.

He was a classic boatie, with his pots of paint and rags soaked in oil. I envied him his seeming lack of care, as he sat in the sunlight on a little stool, rubbing away at the paintwork around the bow. The dinghy was called, poetically, *La Tendresse*. I didn't interrupt him. It was a vision of how life could and indeed should be, when your only worry in life was painting your waterline straight.

I went to find the Mr Kluivert who Roach had told me about, the manager of what looked to be the biggest hotel in town. He was a Dutchman with a manic look to him, and he alternated between English and Spanish when he spoke. He made it clear at once that he didn't want to buy the car.

'Nothing works here,' complained Mr Kluivert. I nodded politely. It was a complaint, along with the tedious jokes about a '*mañana* culture', that Europeans were always making about Central America, usually when they had forgotten quite how inefficient European services could be. We had a mournful cup of coffee together in the foyer of his hotel. He was equally gloomy about my chances of selling the Oldsmobile.

'Try Belize City. If you can't sell it there, you won't sell it anywhere.' Roach had warned me about Belize City. He had told me that it was where every *delincuente* in the country ended up. And he had given me a mournful look to imply that I would probably end up there too.

That night I hit the road on down south to Belize City. I didn't know much about it. In fact all I really knew about the whole country was that Aldous Huxley had once described Belize as 'the armpit of Central America' – and he was the only one of that Thirties generation of writers to make it this far south of the Mexican border.

There were big sand crabs scuttling across the road, lured onto it by the tarmac still hot from the sun. My headlights would pick up their silhouettes as they danced in front of me. It was an image from hell. I pinballed morosely down the road, wheeling from side to side to avoid the potholes and trying to squash any crabs unwise enough to get in my way.

Somewhere along the coast, the engine went. I didn't know what was wrong, but I wasn't going to find out this late at night. I slept in the car, with all the windows open so that the breeze came through. I could hear the distant howler monkeys in the jungle. Even someone as botanically ignorant as me could tell that the forest was changing – from the scrubland of the Yucatan to a thicker, more luxurious mix.

Next morning I discovered one of the fan belts had broken; there seemed to be several. Miraculously, it was one of the few mechanical supplies I'd bothered to pick up before the journey, in some distant echo of the *South American Handbook* mentality. A taxi-driver doing a dawn run up the coast helped me with the belt change. 'Belize City? You won't sell that car anywhere in Belize City. Maybe in Corozal.'

I told him I had just been there.

I was right by a turning to a Classic Maya temple site called Altun Ha. It was a reminder of one reason why I had wanted to come to Belize, for this was the Maya heartland where they had flourished during their Classic Period from around AD 250–900: many of their most impressive cities were here or in neighbouring Guatemala and Honduras. I had always dreamed of seeing the great temples rising up through the jungle, but the imperative of selling the car had diverted me and become overriding.

Altun Ha was a relatively minor site but still idyllic, as if a team of Hollywood carpenters had just rigged and dressed it as a location: a perfectly formed small temple, set in long grass, with a white horse grazing and some fabulous birds flying near by.

Against this backdrop, the car looked like it could be in a television ad. I had got it cleaned and waxed in Corozal. It was asking to be bought. 'Dammit,' I felt like telling prospective punters, 'if I had the money, I'd buy it myself.'

It certainly looked better than I did. My clothes hadn't been washed for a while and I was beginning to get a sticky feeling down the spine where my shirt was clamming up to the car seat. I had ill-advisedly used some Mexican peroxide to bleach my hair and was wearing a cheap pair of 'human fly' sunglasses to keep the glare out of my eyes.

Next to a funeral parlour back on the main road was a shack selling 'beans and rice'. There were two main dishes in Belize: 'beans and rice' or 'rice and beans'; it took me a while to realise that these were genuinely different. It was washed down with some of the filthiest coffee I had ever drunk.

My stomach was still trying to assimilate breakfast as the Oldsmobile and I rolled into Belize City. It was still reasonably early and I hit what must have passed for rush-hour traffic. It felt more like a town than a city, and a shanty town at that, from what I could see: the place was built on a swamp and there were houses on stilts, with deep irrigation canals running between the roads.

I had no plan and 'no particular place to go', in the words of the Chuck Berry song. There was no central square, in the way of a Mexican town, that was alluring enough to stop in and there was an air of menace on the streets, with groups of youths hanging around street corners and eyeing up passers-by.

Navigating aimlessly, I found myself in a more suburban sector – bigger houses, still with canals lining the roads. I was driving one-handed, letting the power-steering do the work as the Oldsmobile swung around the grids of canals.

Maybe the early start or the 'beans and rice' had distracted me, but on one perfectly normal corner I miscalculated and rolled the car into a canal as if I were parking it. One side of the car lurched into the water and it balanced on the edge.

I spent about five minutes just sitting in the car and cursing the day I had ever seen the stupid Oldsmobile in the first place. Then, gingerly, I got out.

'Hello,' said a very English voice, 'do you need any help?' A pink-faced young Englishman was looking down at me from the window of one of the houses opposite.

Richard was an unlikely guardian angel: in his mid-twenties and with his blazer, tie and slacks, he looked like he belonged on a golf course near Basildon, not in Belize City. He was working for Barclays Bank who had interests in Belize. Not only did he use his own car to pull the Oldsmobile out of the canal – I splashed around at the back trying to help – but he then invited me into the house for a much-needed shower and some food.

His rented house was obsessively neat. He lived alone. There were some Desmond Bagley novels on a shelf and a few old copies of *The Economist*. Over a British breakfast (I had forgotten what eating cereal out of packets was like), I told him a suitably abridged version of my story in trying to sell the Oldsmobile. He was appalled by what seemed to him a prime example of 'fecklessness' and by my complete lack of any remaining cash. However he kindly lent me some money to get by.

I cleaned the mud and weeds off the back of the Oldsmobile and headed back into town to see if I could drum up any business. There was a scrappy crossroads and swing bridge where the local youths hung around and passed the time of day. I got talking to a guy with a shaved head and a black coral earring called Bob. Like most of the others, he professed to be a Rastafarian of sorts, even if he didn't have the locks. Bob was not pleased when I questioned whether you could be a true Rasta without the hair. 'I and I knows what is true and what is not true,' he barked. He was not offended enough to refuse the offer of a cup of coffee in the flea-bitten bar across the way.

A friend of his came over and joined us. He was an even less likely Rasta, with blonde hair over an unhealthy ashen skin. I asked Bob about it after he'd left. 'His father came from Babylon,' he explained.

Bob was totally uninterested in my car or my prospects of selling it. 'Maybe you sell it, maybe not,' he shrugged. His only interest seemed to be in whether it had a radio-cassette player. He drove a block or so in the car with me and fingered the tapes: one in particular took his fancy – a lightweight cover version of 'Ring My Bell' by Anita Ward that I had picked up from some discount store in El Paso at the start of my trip. I was embarrassed about it, if the truth were told, but it had a trilling chorus that could satisfyingly cut through the heart when driving.

Bob looked me in the eye. 'Give me this,' he said. It was certainly upfront. I didn't care much about it anyway, so I let him have it and he walked away.

Disco was big in Belize, even among the most righteous of the Rastas. Some of those offloaded records from Chetumal must have seeped down into the national consciousness. I heard a lot of it as I ploughed my lonely furrow among the taxi drivers of the city, either on their radios or blaring out of the street stalls. There were tapes of John Travolta's *Grease* all over the place; they called it '*Vaselina*' in Spanish.

I left the car in what I figured was a conspicuous place, with a large 'FOR SALE' note, and walked around touting for business. It was a slow process, as everyone wanted to talk for a while before telling me they didn't have any money.

An old clapperboard church was a haven of peace, away from the disco music, the taxis, the touts and the smell of fried chicken and lobster. At midday it was cool and empty. The only noise as I walked past the pulpit and the pews, each with a sampler cushion on, were the big fans overhead and the sound of my cheap and heavy Russian camera banging around my neck.

I left through the large porch. To my surprise I saw Rasta Bob reading the notices. He had not struck me as the church-going type. Out of the corner of one eye I saw he had his friend with the Babylonian blond locks with him. That was before the friend grabbed me from behind so that Bob could start beating the shit out of me. The friend used one hand to hold me in an arm lock and the other to cover my mouth. The first blow hit me in the balls; the next, as I doubled up, in the face; then Bob aimed for my chest in what was presumably intended to be the *coup de grâce*. His hand collided with the metal body of the Russian Zenith camera. He swore violently.

'Give me your money.'

'What money? You know I haven't got any.'

Bob's friend had released my mouth so that I could reply. This also meant that I could now scream for help. A middle-aged couple came around the screen into the porch. The man wore a pork-pie hat and wide linen shirt.

'What's happening?' he said in alarm.

Bob gave a last despairing grab at the camera strap around my neck, but I managed to twist in his friend's arms and give a good vicious kick at his knee. Then the two of them ran out. The middle-aged couple were solicitous – and shocked. It was not unusual for muggings to happen in Belize City. 'But in a church!' exclaimed the woman. 'These people have no respect.'

They cleaned me up at a house near by. I had blood running

from a cut above one eye. The blood was still dripping down my face intermittently as I drove back up the highway to Corozal, on what would now have to be my last tank of petrol.

What with the blood, the shock and trying to dodge the crabs – I didn't feel like hurting another living creature now – I kept hitting potholes. It was like being in the dodgems as the car lurched into every little hole. It started to rain. There was only one thing to do. I had saved it for any dire and nihilistic emergencies: my Sex Pistols tape, 'No Fun', at full volume. Was it my imagination or did the crabs try to get out of my way even faster as they heard Steve Jones's blistering guitar runs, fuelled on amphetamines and delinquency?

No fun, my babe, no fun – no fun to hang around feeling that same old way.

No fun to hang around freaked out for another day. No fun!

*

'¿*Chingada madre*? What the fuck happened to you?' asked Roach, after one look at my sorry state. He gave me a drink. It didn't help. I was in a bad way, and not just because my body hurt: I felt stupid and a failure.

I lay on my bed in Roach's flophouse bedroom and watched the ceiling fan go round for hours. I had no money. No one wanted the car, which was falling apart anyway. Jesus, even I wouldn't buy it and I knew nothing about cars. I was back in Corozal, without even enough money to buy another tank of petrol. I had bites all over my body. This was endgame. I remembered Aldous Huxley's comment that Belize (or British Honduras as it had then been) was 'a place that is definitely the end of the world'.

There was a luxury hotel close by along the coast, called the Don Quixote. I roused myself out of depression and torpor to drive down there to see if I might find a rich buyer. When I had mentioned this to Mr Kluivert in Roach's bar and asked if he thought it was a good idea, he was less than encouraging, in his flat, neutral Dutch accent: 'You will never sell that car. Get used to the idea. But you can give me a lift. I want to see Max.'

Max was the manager of the hotel. I had heard about him. He was a Canadian with red hair and the allegedly fiery temperament that goes with it. When we arrived, he was serving up lunchtime drinks to a few ex-pats: the men had hair on the back of their wrists; the women laughed too loudly. They were not about to buy a car from some guy with peroxide-blond spiky hair and human fly sunglasses. Under normal circumstances I would have left straight away.

But Max intrigued me. He wore a bright Hawaiian shirt that did nothing for his redhead's naturally white complexion. However, he was wiry and muscular; he also had a manic energy that reminded me of Malcolm McLaren, the Sex Pistols manager. He gave me a Don Quixote Hotel T-shirt because my clothes were so filthy. And he offered me a margarita. Never had I needed a free drink so much.

I managed to get Max to one side and explained my predicament.

'It's obvious,' he said, as if to an idiot. 'Take the car down to the beach. Pour gas over it. Torch it. And claim the insurance.'

'There is no insurance.'

'In that case you're fucked. Have another margarita.'

Back at Roach's bar, I played pool with some guys until it got dark. One kid had a black coral earring and a wide toothy gin. Roach beckoned me over to the bar. He whispered confidentially: 'Those are bad guys. *Delincuentes y drogados*, delinquents and drug users. You get them in Belize. Don't hang around with them.' He meant well but I was past caring; it seemed anyway a bit rich for a Jamaican to be complaining about drug cultures.

The guy with the earring was called Joshua. He suggested that we go off, do some drugs and find some girls at a brothel he knew. In my current state, this seemed a remarkably good idea, even if they only wanted me along for my car.

I drove them to a house on a side of town I hadn't been to before. As we went in, Donna Summer's 'Bad Girls' was belting out of the speakers; this was either too kitsch to be true or just part of this week's consignment of bad disco from Chetumal:

> Hey mister, have you got a dime?
> Mister, do you want to spend some time?
> I got what you want, you got what I need,
> I'll be your baby, come and spend it on me.

There seemed to be very little sex happening but a good deal of drink and drugs. Joshua rolled a joint so large that even Bob Marley would have taken his time getting through it; another kid had amyl nitrate. The girls sold beers, 'rice and beans', 'beans and rice', and fried chicken. It was more like café than a bordello.

Not having been to a brothel before, I didn't know what to expect. At first it seemed like one of those teenage parties where you don't know anyone, so stay drinking too much on a sofa while the strangers around you have a good time.

With no money left, I wasn't in any case much of a prospective customer. I explained this to a girl called Maria Julia: she was darker than most of the other girls, with jet-black skin and laughing eyes. She wore an orange bikini top with a wraparound skirt. On many girls it would have looked garish; against her black skin it looked fabulous. I had a drink and told her so. I started talking a lot – about the car, about the mess I was in, about music. She wanted to see the car.

By the soft light of the tropical night, the Oldsmobile looked good: the dents were hidden and the turquoise shone with a phosphorescence.

'*Qué carrito,*' murmured Maria Julia, 'What a car! Maybe you just like it too much to sell? If I were you, I'd keep it.'

I switched on the ignition so I could show off the electric windows and the tape player. The sidelights attracted the mosquitoes, so I switched them off.

When we kissed in the dark, her mouth had a sweet saltwater taste, with the smokiness of tobacco. Jesus, it was a good feeling.

She asked if I wanted to stay the night with her in the house. I felt English and embarrassed and young: '*Tengo que regresar al pueblo con los chicos,* I'm meant to be taking the guys back to town,' I muttered. She pointed to said *chicos,* who were sitting on the porch steps passing a joint around; some were already comatose. They were clearly not going anywhere.

'And also,' I blurted out, 'you know I haven't got any money.' She just laughed.

'*¿No te gustan las negritas*? Don't you like black girls? They're better at sex. *Es científico,* it's scientifically proven.'

I wasn't about to disagree, or in a position to. She took me to her room, which was so small the bed almost filled it. I brought up some tapes from the car. We played Bob Marley. What happened next was 'private and also very rude', as Ian Dury used to sing. It was certainly worth driving 5,000 miles through Mexico for.

I couldn't sleep afterwards. I could see the outlines of the trees through Maria Julia's flimsy curtains. The windows were open and a mixture of reggae and cheap disco were coming up from the streets. It was three in the morning. Some birds were already singing.

I felt a sense of liberation. Why worry about the fucking car? What did it matter that in a week's time I was due to start college in England and now didn't have enough money to get home? *Que sera sera.* Maybe I'd just get stuck in Belize for the rest of my days. Right now, that didn't seem such a bad idea. I would have given the car away to spend another night with Maria Julia, or just smoke a cigarette with her on the balcony again and watch the ends burn down together.

*

In the morning, from that same balcony, I could see the waterfront. The same guy I had seen the week before was still painting the waterline on his boat. I went for a coffee at the bar. Roach looked at me with deadpan eyes. Mr Kluivert was there.

'I've been thinking,' said Mr Kluivert. 'I might buy your car after all.'

Later that same day, and before he could change his mind, we were sitting in limbo, in the no man's land between the two frontiers of Belize and Mexico, waiting in the Oldsmobile before the Mexican guards waved us through.

Mr Kluivert was nervous and fidgeting. I hoped he wasn't regretting his impulse buy. He had said it was for his wife, but it was obvious he had bought it for himself.

The Dutchman asked me for a cigarette. I never normally had any, let alone gave them away, but I was feeling expansive. And suddenly rich.

'So,' asked Mr Kluivert, 'what are you going to do now?'

'Study literature. At university.' I knew from experience that saying 'study English' meant nothing, indeed was viewed as a sign of imbecility. Didn't I speak the language already?

Mr Kluivert's reaction was not much better: 'Literature!' he spluttered. 'What is the point of that? What is the *reason* for that?' He wound down the electric windows of his new car and fastidiously tipped the ash onto the asphalt, rather than dirty the car's ashtray. Clearly the Oldsmobile had found that 'one careful owner' it had needed all its life.

He played with the electric window again and adjusted his driver's seat. 'You don't strike me as a teacher, Hugo. And what else are you going to do if you study literature?'

We were waved forward by the guys at the Mexican border before I could answer. They hadn't noticed that we had changed places in no man's land and that while I had driven us out of Belize, Mr Kluivert was now at the wheel. It was his car. I had even signed an affidavit for him.

Mr Kluivert had been impressed when I had outlined the plan. I was leaving Belize in the same car I had arrived, so my passport could be cross-stamped and I was free to do so. He was now entering Mexico in what had become his own car and his passport would be stamped as such. Later that same day he would leave Mexico, again with the same car, as to be expected. And when he re-entered Belize it didn't matter what they stamped on his passport (if they even did – he was friendly with the guards) because he lived there anyway. Meanwhile I was entering Mexico without a car, as a mere passenger – and would leave as such, in just a short while.

Maybe Mr Kluivert was right and I should forget literature. A life of petty crime could be more profitable – and fun, if I was this good at working the angles. I had a wedge of cash in my moneybelt that Mr Kluivert had counted out for me in no man's land: over a thousand dollars, not much of a profit for endless months of travel but better than a smack in the mouth.

I took one last look at the Oldsmobile as I walked away: other peoples' cars always looked better than your own, and already I was forgetting the bad times and remembering that first day when I'd driven south of the border with Steve Miller playing 'Take the Money and Run'; it still looked the fabulous first car that it had been. Even one of the border guards stroked the Cadillac fins.

*

Once back in Mexico, I didn't hang around. A quick internal flight to Mexico City, where I repaid my debts to the car mechanic, Saúl (he got the Zenith camera), and to Jesús and his family, both in cash and with a fiesta of a lunch at which I got mariachis to play for us; then I bought a cash-discounted ticket back to Europe.

During the long hours in transit, I got to thinking more about Kluivert's question, which condensed down to: 'Why Literature? Why not life?' What with getting the car through Mexico, I had given little thought to university, let alone whether there was any point to the study of English.

But oddly the journey, however visceral, had confirmed my hunch that it was the right thing to do. Books mattered because they led readers to places they would not otherwise have dreamed of going, not only geographical places, but also places of the spirit and the emotions.

The conquistadors would never have left Spain for the New World if their heads had not been full of wild romances, of tales of chivalry and confrontation with a strange enemy, however different their actual confrontation with the Aztecs turned out to be. Livingstone only went to Africa because he was influenced by the colourful tales of the traveller Robert Moffat. Likewise Graham Greene was tempted there by reading *King Solomon's Mines* as a child ('without a knowledge of Rider Haggard, would I have been drawn later to Liberia?'). Such accounts, however fictional, were more powerful in luring the traveller than any simple guidebook.

I had only chosen to go to Mexico because of the stories I had read about it, even if those stories had been by long-dead writers of the 1930s who painted a picture of a country barely recognisable from the one I had travelled through.

It is only in the disjunction between what we expect and what we find that the experience of a foreign land is forged. Which is why travel books can be so much more powerful than is often acknowledged by their readers.

*

I fell asleep on the final plane trip back to Europe. When I woke up, I got talking to the girl next to me. She was older, in her late twenties, and had been 'Teaching English as a Foreign Language' (TEFL) around South America and Mexico since leaving college. Her name was Flic, presumably for Felicity. She had that slightly sad air I'd noticed in others I'd come across doing TEFL: the initial liberation of escaping to an exotic foreign clime with money in their pocket turning to indifference as they found themselves years later doing the same thing, for the same money, but just in different places. Now she was spinning back to England without really knowing what was going to happen next.

But she had some interesting stories about South America,

particularly the Andes, which intrigued me. I had grown up on Tintin in South America (*Prisoners of the Sun*) and had a vision of waterfalls, Inca temples and llamas spitting in your face.

And she was pretty, in a quiet way.

'There are still plenty of undiscovered ruins out there, you know,' she said.

'Why doesn't anyone try to find them?'

She shrugged, with the ease of a hispanophile. 'Maybe nobody has the time.'

As we landed, my head was already full of dreams of finding that time.

PART 2: NOW

Travelin' light, we can catch the wind;
We can go to paradise, maybe once, maybe twice.

J. J. CALE, 'TRAVELIN' LIGHT'

RETURNING

I 'm flying into Belize again, tracing the coastline. The inland
swamps are the turgid colour and viscosity of oil paints; only a
thin strip of land separates them from the startlingly clear blue
waters of the Caribbean.

And so I'm back. And everything's changed, and nothing's
changed. Thirty years in the blink of an iguana's eye.

I've always thought that time was not linear, but lay draped
in long swathes of material. Sometimes it stretches smooth and
uninterrupted, but there are times in life when it folds over and
some long-past moment when you were the same person presses
against you. And this is just such a moment.

Back at a place when I was just eighteen. And now I'm forty-
eight. In the last six months I've lost my marriage, my house and
much of my money. I'm dislocated. I don't have an Oldsmobile
98 to sell but a new life to find. I can't remember a time when I
was so up in the air. Or perhaps I can.

*

The streets around Belize city centre are empty. It's a Saturday, a shopping day, but the shops are closed. It's also midday and there are no shadows.

The old swing bridge by the crossroads is still as I remember it, but with just a pathetic cluster of hustlers to either side. Whenever I had crossed it on my first visit, I'd felt like a rugby forward making my way upfield through a whole opposing team. Now there are just three hangers-around to waylay me: the first beckons from a doorway, opening his coat like a flasher – 'whatever you want, mon, I got it'; the next gives me that intense fuck-off look I recognise from crack addicts; the third takes a drag from the last stub of a joint and passes it to me to hold in a gesture of false amiability.

I recognise very little else – except for the old Kingdom Hall where I was mugged. The old clapperboard building has now been deconsecrated and become, to my amusement, the home of the Belize Tourist Authority.

A friendly middle-aged woman comes bustling up the empty street and I discover what's happening: it's a national holiday, Independence Day, and there's a parade of most of the population snaking its way around the other side of town. Pauline wears a baseball hat and a tattoo peeking out from the top of her low-cut T-shirt. She tells me how to cross town to see the parade, but since this means going through the canal district, I should remove my watch and hide my money. 'What about my gold teeth?' I ask. She laughs. Locals are always more paranoid about crime than tourists. And I remember the canal streets as charming.

But it's a long walk in the midday sun and it's day one of my return, so I find a taxi: a resplendent silver Pontiac Parisienne that comes round the corner at me like a fish through water. The driver, Bailey, is avuncular, relaxed, a man who can smoke while driving. I ask him how old the car is.

'1985. A Canadian drove this all the way down from Canada. Then he sold it to me.'

The Canadian had obviously known about the four-door market in Belize. The car has that big-seat feel I remember from the Oldsmobile. You could fit a drum kit in front of the passenger.

I warm to Bailey; he's in his fifties, knows the city and its ways. I tell him about the Oldsmobile. 'Two-door.'

He laughs. 'Yeah, that sure was a big mistake.'

I'm also beginning to feel pleased I took the taxi. The graffiti on the canal-street section we drive through is menacing – 'Don't Change Monkey. Fuck You Black Dog ! – and there are belligerent young men on the corners.

We find a spot on the main avenue and wait for the Independence Day parade to pass. Opposite us is a big pure-blooded Maya guy in a ponytail, with tattoos down his arm; the man next to him wears a T-shirt saying 'I'm great in bed, I can sleep all day'; a hummingbird flutters around the frangipani on the central reservation.

The heat is intense and I'm both jet-lagged and travel-lagged, so the floats when they arrive have a hallucinatory intensity, with super-saturated colours: fifty little girls dressed as fairies in matching and sparkling polka-dotted nylon dresses march by to the beat of an erratic drum; they are followed by the beautiful Miss Belize Past and Miss Belize Present, queens of the carnival in brilliant satin, who wave to the crowd from a float that looks like Thomas the Tank Engine. An athletic guy in tight red and yellow lycra, dressed as a barnyard cock and strutting his splayed legs, gets a very vocal response from the crowd, particularly the ladies.

Some way down the lists comes a more sombre note, with floats imploring that 'the violence be stopped', and placards against the spread of HIV and Aids, with three giant plastic condoms borne along on their own platforms, in pride of place.

It's too much to take in. I'm not ready yet.

*

I woke up to a thin grey light streaming in off the sea. It had rained during the night, heavily, and the dawn coming into the corner bedroom of the old dilapidated hotel by the seafront had a weary, beaten-up quality. In the distance were a few party-goers sheltering under a bandstand by the sea, still smoking and drinking. It was the hangover after Independence Day and I wasn't feeling that good myself.

Not that the intervening thirty years since I was last here hadn't been deeply satisfying. Most of what I wanted when I left Mexico had happened – in some ways, far more: I had become a film-maker and taken expeditions to the Himalaya, to Kilimanjaro and to the Andes – and in the Andes I had taken further expeditions to find some of the pre-Columbian ruins that were already gripping my imagination at eighteen; I had also become a writer and published books on those travels in Peru and the mountains of India. Four years of my life had been spent making an ambitious ten-hour series on the history of rock and roll, for which I'd met and interviewed all those musicians I had carried round in the Oldsmobile on old cassette tapes. I had fallen in love more often than I should have, and a fifteen-year-old marriage had produced three wonderful children, even if it had just ended.

But it was still not easy getting up. I couldn't help feeling that in some obscure way I was back where I started. And why had I come back? Partly to complete an interrupted journey. To find something that I might not have realised or recognised the first time around. And partly, of course, to reconnect with who I was when I had made the journey in the first place.

Only the lure of an illicit pleasure got me out of bed. On my travels over the years since Mexico, I had often made a point of staying in a cheap hotel near a luxury one; not out of hair-shirt austerity, a reminder of how simply I was living, but so that I could illegally use the smarter hotel's swimming pool.

From the Imperial Hotel in Delhi to the Mondrian in Los Angeles, I had busked myself past security. Even in Moscow, where a series of ferocious hotel *babushka* patrolled each step of the process, issuing tickets for both towels and obligatory 'pool slippers', I had slipped my way through. Nothing was more enjoyable than to wander into a luxury hotel as if you owned it, head straight for the pool and immerse yourself before anyone asked any questions.

It appealed to me because of the front needed to escape the vigilance of doormen and surly swimming-pool attendants. They were gatekeepers and, just as at eighteen, I always found the prospect of beating any system irresistible. Plus it was hardly stealing – I was just using a bit of water space and using it well, unlike most of the business guests who were no doubt too fat, pampered or busy to swim at all.

So the Radisson on the seafront, near to the lighthouse and my own downmarket hotel, was a natural lure. By the time I got there, the sun had cut through the dawn drizzle and was burning up nicely. Security was lax and I was the only person in the pool; there was a jacuzzi as well. Things were looking up.

The bar beside the pool was playing a radio phone-in show

called 'Wake Up Belize', hosted by a young DJ called Euan 'Mose' Hyde. He combined excellent musical taste in roots reggae with a political aggressiveness that would not have been out of place on the *Today* show or Larry King. As I listened idly to Mose over a poolside breakfast of chilled orange juice and proper espresso, I became engrossed.

Some of the enthusiasm for the Independence Day celebrations I had witnessed was because Belize had only finally been given its independence from Britain in 1981, two years after I had been there. It seemed extraordinary that such colonialism should have continued so long; after all, the rest of Central America had won independence from Spain in the previous century.

Self-rule had not been an unmitigated success – Belizeans had used their new-found democratic powers to boot out each under-performing government at every election since 1981. Mose's aggressive style of interviewing reflected the dissatisfaction felt by many Belizeans at the failure of their politicians to deliver.

Today's victim was the Minister of Sport, whom Mose accused of misappropriating millions of dollars given to the country annually by FIFA: 'So where are the pitches?' he asked. 'Where can the youth get training? It's a lot of money to have nothing to show for it.'

The minister floundered and tried bonhomie: 'I always enjoy fighting with you, Mose.'

But Mose did not let this put him off his stride: 'The fact is, Minister, that if you fail, you will be judged by history, not me.'

And this was just the Minister of Sport – I would have loved to have heard him with the top men in power. He was so good I decided on impulse to head over to the radio station and catch Mose after the show. This was not something I would have done thirty years ago – but then I had got used to cutting to the chase when producing films. And Belize was a small country, so people should be easy to find.

Bailey was outside on the taxi-rank polishing his Pontiac Parisienne. After the rain and with the sun reflecting off the sea, the silver paintwork was already gleaming. It turned out he knew Mose personally and could take me to KREM Radio, 'Belize's first independent radio station'.

It lay just off the canal zone. There was considerable security around the entrance, for good reason: just the week before, shots had been fired into Mose's compound and his car fire-bombed with a Molotov cocktail after he went after corrupt elements of the government on air.

We had been listening to the show on Bailey's in-car stereo as we drove over and now heard Mose on the security guard's radio as he was signing off: 'We urge you all to stand strong, stand firm.' He segued into a Bob Marley song, then wandered onto the balcony by the studio and I could see him, a slight man in his thirties, wearing a beret.

There were no preambles. His manner was as direct with me as it was on air: 'Let me tell you, the three major problems facing Belize are with the utilities, police abuse and corr-*up*-tion.' He said corruption as Fela Kuti sang it, with a stress on the '*up*'.

'The problem with utilities is that privatisation has created very cold institutions, with no moral obligation to people. They cut the poor off, then make them pay high reconnection fees. And the police abuse is exacerbated by the gang violence, which is "the painful reality of our urban existence" here.' This last phrase sounded both poetic and well used.

'We're on the trans-shipment highway of narcotics up to the US. We are, to all intents and purposes, a "narco-state". The corr-*up*-tion is not so much on the streets – we don't have the *mordida* culture of "the little bite" like they do in Mexico, where everyone's on the take. But higher up, with the politicians, it's a mess.'

He saved his greatest rage for Michael Ashcroft, the billionaire who seemed to have a hand in every business in Belize, from banking to the phone system and the controversial cruise-ship business which was turning the country into a cut-price Florida: 'He's an imperial figure, who's accommodated by our political leaders, a monster that needs to be leashed. He's got all the elected officials by the testicles. And for someone who's so rich and successful, he has a spoilt-child meanness and spite about him – the sort of man who will squash an ant. He'll put equity into a company, then suck the soul out of it with his lawyers.'

I knew already that Ashcroft was litigious, and it was clear that there was an ongoing battle between him and KREM Radio.

I asked Mose about the quite separate recent attempt on his life by unnamed politicians, which he shrugged off: 'It was a warning. These things happen.'

He had to get on to a meeting, but focused on me for the first time as he left. 'Who are you by the way? We just been talkin' and I know nothing about you.'

*

Bailey took me for a cruise along the unusually quiet canal streets of the Southside near by. It was early on Sunday morning and the Independence Day revellers were still in bed.

At first Bailey shot me a familiar line – that the crime here wasn't caused by Belizeans: it was all the Mexicans, Hondurans and Guatemalans who came in, let alone the Colombians who were shipping cocaine into the country as an easy back way into

Mexico and over the unregulated NAFTA border. But then he relaxed into more direct home truths.

'Thing have gone bad in Belize. Ten people were shot around here in just the last couple of weeks.' It was crack that, as in nearby Jamaica, had taken a long-term, low-maintenance drug culture, fond of its Rasta herb, and fired it into something altogether meaner and more violent.

'They get a *fonta* leaf from Mexico, fill it with a mixture of crack and marijuana and smoke it in a pipe. And that *fonta* leaf often has had bad chemicals sprayed on it by the growers.' Given what they were smoking inside the leaf, I was amused at Bailey's concern that the product wasn't organic.

I already knew that things had got worse in Belize City since I had left. When in 1993 Nicolas Roeg chose to film *The Heart Darkness* here – an interesting choice in itself – some dozen of his crew members were mugged.

In the early morning sun, all was looking quiet. Two girls rode by on the same bicycle, one balancing the other on the handlebars.

Bailey looked at them mournfully. 'It's the politicians. That's where the corruption comes from.'

He pulled over so we could talk more easily and told me of a recent case where a senior member of the governing PUP had been killed in a crash on the Northern Highway; his car contained, so rumour had it, various guns, a briefcase full of money and bags of crack. 'And out by the airport they got this big house where they hold parties. They take these young girls, some just fourteen, fifteen, promise 'em a good time, give 'em drugs an tings, and then . . .', he shrugged: 'Some of 'em parties are totally nude.'

We had stopped near one of the city's many small churches. The service was just beginning and I joined the back of the congregation. The Anglican Church of All Saints ('Make a Joyful

Noise to the Lord') was packed. I stood by the door. Boys and girls in red surplices read the lessons. The vicar came down into the middle of the congregation to lead the service. There were prayers for those in need, for the community, for 'all our sick and shut-ins'.

As we drove away Bailey said, 'There's still a lot of religious people here. But it's hard. It's a struggle.'

We passed a discount supermarket called Bottom Dollar ('Come Stretch Yuh Dollar'). Bailey told me that it was owned by 'the third richest man in Belize'.

'The economy's so bad here – we all ha' to *multi-task*.' He almost spat the word out.

*

I was swimming into a cave. After travelling through the cloud forest by the heat of the midday sun, the cold of the dark water came as a shock. The cave entrance was shaped like an hourglass, with a deep pool stretching back inside it, so that as I swam I started to lose the light as well. And the water got colder. It could not have been more different from the Radisson.

This was Actun Tunichil Muknal, 'the cave of the stone sepulchre' on the edge of the Maya Mountains. It was a day's journey from Belize City; I had taken a series of local buses to get here, mostly crammed with schoolchildren, and then found a guide who could lead me inside.

Beyond the entrance to the first cave lay over five kilometers of twisting tunnels linking more cavern systems, many of them flooded, which we now had to penetrate wearing head-torches and helmets. I had never potholed before or wanted to, being more drawn to mountains and the heights than claustrophobia.

But this was an exceptional opportunity, for the strangeness of the swim was taking me deep inside the Maya world.

When I had first come to Belize, the caves had yet to be discovered. It was only in 1986 that some *chicleros*, 'rubber-gatherers', had stumbled across the entrance when walking through these isolated foothills of the Maya Mountains; they showed them to a young geomorphologist called Thomas Miller who was working in the area.

Miller's excitement at what he found must have been intense, but he also knew he lacked the relevant training to capitalise on the discovery. So with commendable patience, he went off to do a PhD in archaeology before returning in 1989 with a further expedition, which this time included cavers. The published account of his discoveries caused a sensation.

For most of the Nineties, Actun Tunichil Muknal was closed to all but specialist archaeologists as the complex was mapped and researched – but after 2000 it was opened to a few carefully trained guides, like my current one, Daniel, a native Belizean.

Daniel had advised me that the rock surface of the cave walls and floor was too abrasive to risk stripping down to swim, and so we surfaced from the pool in dripping clothes and shoes. Water-filled channels led away from us into the dark. Walking chest-deep down them behind Daniel, I tried to imagine what it must have been like for the Maya, entering what they regarded as the spirit world of the caves, their flickering bark torches illuminating the same stalactites and column formations that our head-torches were picking out, and casting similar shadows.

Archaeologists had speculated that the Maya might have modified some of the formations we passed to emphasise certain features: near the entrance, some hollow depressions in the rock face looked like the eye sockets of a skull; there was the distinctive outline of a poised jaguar near by.

The force of the water flowing through the narrow channels was strong and we had to push hard against it, sometimes up to our necks, while also finding our footing on the large littered boulders beneath the water. I was wearing a pair of tough trekking sandals with a good grip, but they were getting trashed by the abrasive rocks and the sheer force of the water pulling them back off my soles. Every so often there was a further short climb up a stretch to another cave system. At one point we passed another entrance letting in light from above, more like a well or '*cenote*', before we began to ascend and find ourselves in wider chambers.

Here Daniel could use his flashlight to illuminate pots that the Maya had placed on ledges to either side of the caves as offerings; an image of the Mexican deity Tlaloc had also been found here. These offerings were preliminaries to the grisly ceremony that was to take place in the centre of the complex.

We came to the main chamber, a cathedral of a rock-space with stalactites and columns. Parts of the ground were so covered by shards of pot that we had almost to tiptoe around them; small holes had been neatly trepanned in the back of the offered pots to release the spirit within, as if they were skulls.

The pottery shards had been left in place on the cave floor because they were embedded in heavy calcite deposits left by the regular flooding, and so extracting them was almost impossible; the archaeologists, with the forbearance and 'future- proofing' that was their most admirable characteristic, had elected to leave the pots in place for a future generation with better tools.

This made it a quite exceptional experience – anywhere else, if the pots had not been removed, they would at least have been fenced off and protected under glass, completely forbidden to the non-archaeological visitor. But here one could still for the while (although I suspected for not much longer) see the caves exactly as they were first left by the Maya at the time of their likely abandonment around AD 959.

Daniel led me around these higher levels of the cave in a complicated dance through the shards of ceramics in the pools, with as much care as earlier we had negotiated the narrow flooded passageways of the lower cave system. My light trekking trousers and surfer's rash vest had at least dried quickly after each immersion in the water; nor was it as cold as I expected in the upper caverns. But the sensory disorientation was extreme. After an hour or so (we spent four hours in the caves in total), I was completely lost; without Daniel I would have certainly been unable to find my way back out. And of course neither radios let alone mobile phones worked this far underground; I couldn't help wondering what would happen if Daniel were to hit his head against a rock or simply got separated from me. Which was not going to happen, but the darkness of the caves encouraged irrational thoughts.

And I thought of those brought in here as human sacrifices, often drugged with enemas or hallucinogenics injected into the bloodstream, for whom the mild disorientation I was experiencing would have been elevated into a shot of intense fear; only the presence of accompanying attendants could have guided and forced them deeper and deeper into the labyrinth, to the place where they would meet their deaths.

Sixteen such victims had been found in the caves, from very young children to adults. Daniel showed me some of their skeletons: skulls pressing up from the calcite deposits like faces through a blanket; a young teenage boy pressed against a wall, who had been left with his hands tied, a horrible, miserable death; most dramatic of all, the full skeleton of a woman with splayed out legs, in a remote, higher cave that was only accessible by ladder. It was unclear whether the legs were splayed deliberately, positioned in such a way that she was offering herself to a deity, or whether the body had been swept down from higher up the cave by the occasional flood waters. Either way, the image unsettled and disturbed me.

Staring at the skeleton of the young woman was a pivotal moment. It was as far as I could go within the cave system, but also as far as I could empathise with the Maya. Whatever anthropologists might say about 'appreciating cultural difference', the fact remained that this young woman had been brutally murdered, probably when frightened out of her senses on hallucinogenics administered by force. Whatever belief system was in place – and whatever the considerable pressure that the system was under by the time these sacrifices were made, between AD 700–900, the Terminal Classic Period of the Maya as it is sometimes known – nothing could alter that brutality for me.

Daniel saw that I was upset. 'Just think of your own Princess Diana,' he said. 'I saw a Discovery documentary about her. In some ways, she was your own human sacrifice.'

*

For the Maya, human sacrifice seems to have been occasional, unlike the wholesale butchery that was being conducted by the Aztecs further north in Mexico when Cortés arrived. What by the end of the Classic Period seems to have brought them to such extreme measures was the scale of the population explosion. Belize is now a relatively sparsely populated country of less than 250,000 people. In Classic Maya times, it was some four times that number, with a population of over a million.

On leaving the cave system, Daniel and I drove through an empty valley pockmarked by tumuli from early Maya settlements; archaeologists estimate that a population of tens of thousands had lived in just this one valley. Today no one lived there at all.

The Maya were the eco-victims of their own success. Over the millennium of the Classic Period from around AD 250–900, they had carved out city-states in the most unpromising of terrains, the deep jungle of the Petén, and their skilful use of crop rotation had supported an ever increasing population. But even they were unable to sustain this indefinitely. As resources got sparser, Maya skeletons show that they became more and more malnourished.

One theory holds that the careful agricultural balance needed in the rainforest began to break down. The last patches of virgin forest were stripped away and the topsoil destroyed by over-farming. There might have been widespread civil unrest – and certainly warfare between the various city-states competing for ever diminishing resources. Human sacrifice may have increased as a way for rulers to appease both the gods and their populace.

What we do know is that by AD 950 almost all the great cities of the Classic Period in the central jungles had been abandoned; instead, the centre of Maya civilisation moved closer to the coast and particularly to Yucatan, where I had seen some of their very late sites on my first journey.

It had taken a thousand years after the collapse of the Classic Maya civilisation for the forests to grow back; the romantic image of Maya temples covered in greenery, and of a civilisation who lived at one with nature in a way we do not, was a completely false one, even if it did help sell Body Shop bath oils. The Maya cities were in all likelihood as overbuilt as the Los Angeles conurbation.

It was natural for me to be attracted to the Maya remains in

Belize – after years spent studying the Incas in Peru, I was drawn to the pre-Columbian civilisations, but also aware of the deep popular misconceptions about them. And many of these misconceptions about the Maya had only just been dispelled by scholars in the last few years.

This was another prime reason for coming back. I had only begun to scratch the surface of the Maya civilisation on my first visit, and since that first visit some remarkable discoveries had been made, both in places like the Actun Tunichil Muknal cave and deciphering the Maya script. Those discoveries had opened up the Maya mindset in a remarkable and unexpected way.

*

I rode out to another remote Maya site close to the border with Guatemala, called Xunantunich (pronounced '*shoo-nan-too-nich*'), where again considerable work had been done in the last few years. This time my guide was a full-blooded Rasta, an ex-jockey called Ali of about my age who had cut his locks twice in his life but still boasted an extravagant head of hair. I had plenty of time to study it as I rode behind him. It was a perfect day to be on a horse: sunny but with a light wind coming up from the plains. As befitted a man who had won every riding cup in Belize during his time on the turf, Ali was occasionally impatient at my slowness, but impressed that I had seen Aswad play live at the Meanwhile Gardens.

He told me a little about himself as the horses meandered at my desultory pace across the grassland. He had three children, like me, but both his sons were now dead: one as a child from illness, the other from a more recent riding accident; only his daughter had survived and she was living with a policeman. Ali snorted, sounding like his horse: 'Who'd have t'ought a Rasta would end up with a policeman as his son-in-law?'

We were riding through farmland made lush by the rainy season: tropical cedars, palms, ceibas and giant guanacaste trees dotted the grassland. When he got bored, Ali forced me into a reluctant gallop. The white cattle egrets showed up with startling intensity against the green as we crested a rise, and white peacock butterflies scattered under the horses' feet. Spiny iguanas, startled by our sudden approach, slithered through the grass towards the nearby river. Not a single modern house could be seen on the horizon; only the principal temple of Xunantunich was visible on a faraway hill. Any pleasure at seeing it was mitigated by the thought of how saddle-sore I would be by the time we got there.

The placid and beautiful landscape of the Mopan valley we were riding through had an important effect on Maya studies. After the Second World War, a young British archaeologist called Eric Thompson worked here; he was later to become the leading Mayanist of his generation.

It was Thompson who promoted the vision that was still current when I had first come to Mexico – of the Maya as a Greek-style civilisation of city-states who lived in relative harmony, sharing their impressive knowledge of astronomy and time-keeping: the star-gazers of Mesoamerica. His experience of these gentle and fertile grasslands may have helped him to that view.

Thompson was awed by the precision of Maya time-keeping, far more accurate than any contemporary Western equivalents. He was also influenced strongly by the fact that while the dates on their stelae had been deciphered and their complex system of time-keeping accurately described (the so-called 'Long Count'), the 'narrative glyphs' on the stelae had not yet been translated and it was thought never would be.

But while I had been away, much had changed. The story of how those glyphs were finally translated in the years since Thompson was one of the great intellectual achievements of the late twentieth century; Thompson's preconceptions had been overturned by a maverick alliance of American and Russian scholars, like the reclusive Yuri Knorosov in St Petersburg, who helped make the vital breakthrough without ever visiting a Maya site in his life.

Up until the decipherment of the Maya glyphs, the archaeologists had been in a not much better position than I had been at Palenque thirty years before, scrabbling around in the rainforest to see what evidence lay on the ground, or just under it; but now they could survey the whole panorama of Maya history from the temple rooftops.

The glyphs revealed that far from being the peaceable Greeks of the Mesoamerican world, as I remembered hearing when I first visited their ruins, the 'storehouses' of peaceful learning from which other more bellicose cultures could draw, the Maya cities were constantly at war with one another.

Stone stelae standing at each site told the story of how Tikal, the most romantic of all their sites, lost in the Guatemalan jungle until the nineteenth century, had been locked for centuries in bitter combat with another city, Calukmal; at one point Tikal had almost completely shut down for a century after a particularly vicious attack, which had left Caracol, a city lying in modern-day Belize, the licence to grow in its stead. The tomb I had once visited at Palenque of Pacal, the tall king in his sarcophagus at the base of the temple, was only so richly decorated because he had led a renaissance of the city after it had been virtually annihilated by its neighbours.

Across the whole Classic Maya world, stretching across Central

America from Belize through Guatemala to Honduras, the narrative glyphs revealed a tale in which the construction of monumental buildings was mixed with intrigue, murder and brutality. The Maya rulers were given to penile blood-letting, human sacrifice – often throwing victims into the deep wells, or '*cenotes*', formed in the limestone peninsula of the Yucatan – and the decapitation of rival kings, all habits of their Mexican cousins, the Teotihuacán civilisation and later the Aztecs.

Indeed, the Maya were far more like their Aztec counterparts than had at first been thought, with the same concerns for endless warfare and appeasing the gods through sacrifice. The glyphs even revealed that there had been direct contact between the two civilisations: representatives from Teotihuacán near modern-day Mexico City had visited both Palenque and Tikal, and in the Actun Tunichil Muknal cave I had explored with Daniel, a slate had been found with the image of Tlaloc, the goggle-eyed, snaggle-toothed and demandingly warlike deity I was familiar with from Central Mexico.

In the cave there had also been a slate engraved with a stingray, iconic for the Maya as they used its barb for ritual blood-letting: women would pierce their tongue, while men pierced their genitals – although it occurred to me that archaeologists were too polite to wonder just how much blood one could actually draw from a penis.

Ali and I came to a crossing over the Mopan River; a hand-cranked ferry took both us and the horses over to the other side. The horses were used to the river roaring beneath them. Then it was a short ride of about a mile up to Xunantunich, set on its hilltop with commanding views over the countryside.

Like so many other Maya sites, Xunantunich was still being cleared and restored; a magnificent frieze had only recently been uncovered in 1993 on the west side of the Castillo, the principal building, a reminder that the site would have been far more richly decorated in its heyday. Around the central plazas, the main temples and the ball court, which had been cleared, there were many still unrestored buildings extending into the forest.

The view from the top of the Castillo was compelling: the rolling green hills of the Cayo stretched away in waves, hills that reminded me oddly of the view from the Hog's Back in Surrey, so English and understated were they, albeit with a few more palms and tropical cedars.

Was it any wonder that Eric Thompson after working here should have formulated his theory of the Maya as wise old men living in the forests? And that writing after a time of warfare in Europe, the ideal of a peaceful pre-Columbian society should have been so attractive?

If like Stephens and Catherwood, the pioneering nineteenth-century explorers, Thompson had come across the Maya in some mosquito-infested corner of the Petén or Chiapas, the deep jungle of the land-locked interior, would he have emerged with such a rosy and influential view of the Maya as this green and pleasant land before me had given him?

I liked sometimes to imagine what would happen if our own civilisation came to an end and Times Square was found in 500 years' time, the billboards faded and grey, the trees from Central Park having spread through the asphalt and ripped it picturesquely to pieces, and the colour tastefully bleached from the neon displays: how peaceful and romantic future archaeologists might find it, a respite from their own roistering times.

And I remembered my own first impressions when I had seen the picturesque ruins of Palenque and the other sites in the Yucatan, and of how I had been drawn to the romantic engravings of

Catherwood and seen them as emblems of a wilderness experience – whereas in fact they were symbols of overpopulation, overproduction and a society, much as our own, completely incapable of sustaining its own environment.

*

'So you're a writer and explorer who travels to lots of faraway countries?' Usually the response in Belize to what I did ranged from the uncomprehending to the more universal 'How can you get away with having such a great job and still be paid for it?'

But William, the self-made businessman who was giving me a lift in a large air-conditioned SUV, was going further: 'What you have to do to be a writer, Hugh, is to make people believe in *every-word-you-write.*' With every one of his own words he pumped the wheel as if to give it heart relief. We were only cruising down the hill to town from my hotel but it was making me nervous.

'*And-what-you-really-really-really* have to do,' pumped William, now looking at me rather than the road, 'is make them want to pay for *every word* you write.'

He was getting evangelical now: 'That's what I've done. I've built up a business selling phone card credit machines to hotels. Did you make a call from the hotel? That was my phone card system you used. Because people want to make calls. Stuck in their hotel rooms, bored and lonely. Do you ever get bored and lonely, Hugh?'

I had an aversion to people using my name the whole time when they had only just met me. 'No,' I said truculently and untruthfully.

'Well many people do. And I've also got a car-parts firm in Belmopan. And you know why that's a success?'

I didn't, but suspected that William was going to tell me.

'Because people [*pump*] want [*pump*] my products. So they pay me.'

William seemed exhausted by the effort it had taken to get this point across. He turned up the car stereo that had been playing a selection of Seventies MOR, which had been the disco soundtrack last time I'd been here: The Cars, Barry Manilow and Queen.

Listening to 'Bohemian Rhapsody' seemed to calm William. He turned his sweating dark-black face to me, his eyes picking up reflections from the town lights that we were now approaching.

Now he spoke more softly: 'You see what you can do with your writing is to take people into a sixth dimension. You know what the first two dimensions are, right?'

He looked at me to check that despite my clear lack of business acumen I was not a complete idiot. 'The third is time. The fourth is memory. The fifth is music. And the sixth? If I need to tell you what the sixth dimension is, you'll never know.'

He stopped the car. We had arrived at the pool hall where I was due to meet Ali. It had been a short drive but a very long journey.

*

'You lookin' for Ali, you meetin' him?' said the barman, when I asked. 'You goin' to have a wild time, mon!'

I had enjoyed the horse-riding with Ali and we had agreed to meet up later to see some of the nightlife in San Ignacio, the local town that was the jumping-off point for the various Maya ruins in the vicinity. Ali was on Rasta time and hadn't shown up yet. But as a retired champion jockey, his reputation preceded him: he was well known in the town's bars, partly because, as I soon saw, he had more front than Blackpool.

Ali had claimed that Belizean girls were 'hard work – they wear T-shirts over their bikinis when they swim, shit like that,' and that European girls were more easy-going. He had a big thing for the English girls who passed through, not least because, unlike me, they were excellent horse-riders. But no discrimination was applied at all in his chat-up technique: within five minutes of arriving, he had propositioned everything in a skirt, regardless of nationality and with equal lack of success. A smattering of foreign travellers passed through the bar, every female one of whom Ali asked to join us for a game of pool; when they refused, he asked the bargirl instead.

With his Rude Boy charm and jockey's small but wiry physique, Ali carried a certain charisma. We ended up playing pool with two young local lads who were somewhat overawed by the Rasta style with which he potted his shots: fast and loose, while dancing to the intensely loud, rock-steady reggae beat, a cigarette clamped to his lips.

Between us we beat our young contenders and got through a Belikin beer a game, so were well prepared for the next stage of the evening's entertainment: a dance hall on the outskirts of San Ignacio that Ali told me was 'strictly for locals'.

The place was the size of a barn and pumping out ragga music at ferocious volume. A notice on the door declared: 'No gang colours on display. No attitude. No firearms.' Although it was coming up to midnight, this was still early for Belize night-life and the club was almost empty. A video screen was showing close-to-pornographic ragga videos; a group of girlfriends with handbags were watching and dancing together.

For once Ali went shy and it was up to me to ask one to dance. She was darker than most of the locals, pretty and with a short white dress that showed up in the fluorescence; she was also a fabulous dancer and had mastered the ragga style of pumping her hips as she lowered herself, which was not only sexual but also, I couldn't help thinking, murder on the back of the thighs, like skiing.

With some difficulty, given the noise level, I told her that she was a good dancer – it was not the moment to try anything too original – and she said that was despite having had five kids. I said that mothers made the best dancers and she laughed. Conditions were not good for any more sparky or extended conversation, like asking her name; it was like trying to speak in the eye of a storm. A local MC was attempting some uninspired toasting bigger on feedback than inspiration, but we made a good attempt at dancing to the fearsomely loud ragga; or she was at least kind enough to tell me so, as she drifted back to her girlfriends, and that we would have another dance later.

But when that 'later' came, I realised what I had been doing wrong. I saw her with a local going for an ever more exaggerated sexual humping motion as she danced, and this time she was stroking her crotch at the same time. And Jesus, no it couldn't be but it was: her male partner was doing exactly the same, stroking his own crotch as he humped down towards the floor.

Even the most liberated of Englishmen have their limits; it was time to withdraw from the competition, not that I was anyway in the market.

Ali had already retired for some serious smoking. I wandered back down the road under the stars, several Belikin beers to the west and ignoring the worries of paranoid taxi drivers that I would be mugged and left for dead if I didn't take myself under their voluntary embrace. The sound of the ragga echoed behind me as if it were a wild beast trying to break out of the building. The stars were out as I wandered past the small Maya ruin of Cahel Pech.

There was a contradiction at the heart of Belizean culture common to other parts of the Caribbean I had visited, like Jamaica: on the one hand, a strong church-going ethos that valued education and community spirit; on the other, a heavily sexualised dance-hall culture stirred up by drugs and guns.

Hard for the two to mix, but they did. The girls wearing Sunday school best for their morning church services were the same as the ones gyrating so graphically in the dance halls. It was perhaps not surprising that at times Belize seemed a society ill at ease with itself.

*

The power boat curled and whipped around the river bends like a fairground ride. I was holding on to the side rails not so much for the speed, but for those lurches of sudden deceleration when the helmsman spotted anything in the shallows: some elegant northern jacanas, little red-breasted waders, picking their way among the water hyacinths – the Belizeans called them 'the Jesus Christ bird' because they seem to walk on water – or a crocodile submerging quietly as we approached.

We were heading for Lamanai, a remarkable and curious Maya site that had long intrigued me and which lay upriver from Orange Walk; the boat had picked our small party up from the quay just below the town guesthouse. The river was by far the best means to get to Lamanai and was also a way of seeing the rural back country. The warm smell of molasses reached us down the water long before we came upon its source, one of the last surviving sugar-cane factories. Near by, an elegant blue heron stalked the banks, while the bony silhouette of a cormorant extended like another branch from a tree whose leaves had been stripped by the flood water.

Around a few further bends came the sudden vision of a Mennonite community, with its wind-driven pumps and horses by the water. The Mennonites were similar to the Amish in the States, a German-speaking Anabaptist sect who kept to their old *hochdeutsch* rural ways, with no time for electricity or twentieth-century inventions. An old-timer of the hard-line persuasion was walking towards the horses; he pretended not to notice our power boat, as though we were a phantom apparition, like a Maya longboat gliding past him.

The Maya had used this waterway extensively. With no available beasts of burden, the network of rivers that threaded through the jungles of modern-day Belize, Guatemala and Mexico was the only fast way for these obsessive traders to get about. As we entered the wide lagoon where Lamanai was situated, it was clear where the city's prosperity had come from; it was effectively an inland port.

Snail kites were circling some of the finest of Lamanai's buildings, the temples that poked through the treetops lining the lagoon shore. Our small group were the only people there and the experience of wandering around an empty, deserted city was bizarre. Of the estimated 940 stone buildings that had survived (with the presumption of a far greater number of simpler structures that hadn't), only seven had been cleared and partially restored – what archaeologists called 'the central core' – so most of the city was still submerged beneath thick jungle vegetation.

The Temple of the Jaguar Masks was the first I came to; then the High Temple with a sweeping view over the lagoon and surrounding jungle; and most remarkable of all, the Mask Temple, with a large statue at its base, looking uncannily like something the overheated imagination of a video-game designer might conjure up: a face that was open-mouthed, close-lidded and taller than a man.

Four other monumental buildings had been uncovered, but there was still a large acropolis area that had yet to be cleared, let alone the many pyramidal buildings that stretched to the nearby village and were still just looming shapes among the trees. It was a huge site, for Lamanai had enjoyed an unusually long time in which to expand: the first inhabitants had arrived as early as 1500 BC, with the city reaching its peak during the Classic Maya period from AD 250–900 when it had a population of some 40,000.

What made Lamanai almost unique was that alone of the large Maya cities in Belize, it had somehow survived the apocalypse of around AD 900–950 at the end of that Classic Maya period. And that was the reason I had wanted to come here. For why was it that Lamanai continued, flourishing almost, until the arrival of the Spaniards in the sixteenth century, when all the other cities near by had been long abandoned? And even after the Conquest, it was so remote from the centres of Spanish colonial control that Maya Indians continued to live here until AD 1700, an extraordinary continuous occupation of some 3,000 years. Few cities in the world outside of Egypt and Mesopotamia could match that, and certainly none in the Maya world.

Perhaps its long survival was because, although some fifty miles inland, it was a port; we know that even after the near total collapse of their Classic Period cities, the Maya continued to trade around the coast to Yucatan. For that matter, the extent of that Classic Period 'collapse' may have been overexaggerated. Some scholars were beginning to feel that the Maya just moved from the old model of city-states ruled by hierarchical kings to a more mercantile society, less concerned with leaving monumental religious buildings behind and more interested in trade than agriculture –

the sort of shift that occurred in Europe towards the end of the Middle Ages. They may have abandoned their great cities to the jungle, but continued elsewhere.

In the late nineteenth century, the British had moved into this area for the sugar cane and had lived among some of the Maya ruins at Lamanai; I couldn't held speculating what a Victorian British family would have made of such heathen architecture – let alone the howler monkeys – although they would have approved of the Maya enthusiasm for trade.

With its long occupation, the city was an archaeologist's dream, and had been well served by them. In 1980, just after I had left Belize, a Canadian team had uncovered the 'central core' of the site and found an offering of liquid mercury under a limestone slab. Together with some incense burners found on the Mask Temple, this suggested that Lamanai was a place of pilgrimage from around the Maya world. The archaeologists had also excavated a burial site and found to their surprise that the couple within – known as 'the loving couple' – had come from west Mexico, 1,000 miles away, more evidence of the cosmopolitan society that Lamanai had attracted as a Mesoamerican Byzantium.

Sitting on the summit of the High Temple, as much to keep away from the mosquitoes as for the view, I closed my eyes and listened to the noise of the surrounding jungle. Sound recordists I had worked with loved to talk of a 'skyline track', and this was a skyline track in glorious stereo, with a deep sub-woofer. Below the twittering of the trogons and parrots in the nearby trees thudded the wild and unholy bass of the far-off howler monkeys, like a whale moving beneath the jungle floor and occasionally surfacing.

And it came to me why I was so insistently drawn to these pre-Columbian civilisations, why since those firsts nights spent sleeping by the ruins in my car I had gone back again and again to the Inca ruins of Peru – and now had come back to the Maya.

In a world that was over-commodified, over-explored and overrun by the internet and the information explosion, here was something that was still very little understood. We might have begun to translate the Maya glyphs (although we had not managed even that with the Zapotec script or the Inca *quipus*), but we were still just scratching the surface of these alien civilisations, with their radically different view of the world. Literally scratching the surface, as only the archaeologists were ever going to get any real results. And given that for good and bad professional reasons, they paced themselves like snails on Quaaludes, it might take another century before we really started getting answers as to why the Maya collapsed – and what the motor of their civilisation was, their *alma*, their soul.

Maybe my children would come back some day to see the full extent of Lamanai, or Tikal, or Calukmal, or any of the other great sleeping whales of the Mesoamerican rainforest. Meanwhile we could still be as wrong about the Maya as the much derided Eric Thompson was a generation ago, when he described them as peaceful denizens of the forest – just wrong in different ways.

I opened my eyes. In the distance, over the treetops, the solid black sheet of a storm was coming.

The return journey was the wettest I have ever taken. First the rain came down and drenched us. Then further washes of river water flooded the power boat as we bucketed along. Desperate to get home and out of the storm, our helmsman broke every possible health and safety regulation, driving the boat around the bends so fast the gunwales dipped below the waves.

And I thought of another emotive aspect of Lamanai. For once we know what the Maya inhabitants called a city themselves, rather than the fanciful and dull names imposed on other sites (Caracol meaning 'snail' because shells were found there; El Mirador, lamely, because it is indeed good as 'a lookout'). 'Lamanai' is the his-panicised form of *Lama' an/ayin*, the real name, still in use when the Spaniards first arrived: it means 'submerged crocodile'. Like that ancient creature from the time of the dinosaurs, the city had survived several epochal changes.

*

So far I had resisted trying to pin down the past too firmly, keeping away from any old haunts. Only in Belize City had it been unavoidable. But Lamanai was close to Corozal, where I had finally sold the car after those febrile weeks on the lam, and I couldn't resist heading back to see what I could find.

The early morning bus up to Corozal was an express, so I could recline in air-conditioned comfort as it charged the Northern Highway. I had remembered the route as slow and potholed, but now it was unrecognisable, a smooth, fast road. This was where I had swerved the Oldsmobile from side to side trying to hit or avoid the land crabs at night, depending on my mood or state of desperation.

A grizzled American Peace Corps veteran in the seat in front explained: 'This highway is new. The old one got so bad they had to abandon it completely and just start again. Some of those potholes were like bomb craters – a family could live in one. But then what do you expect in a country so trashed it's never had a single railroad?'

We passed a small shack that was under threat from developers. It was plastered with signs saying 'KEEP OFF! THIS BELLONGS TO JOHN!' Further on were a row of used car lots and breakers yards. I daydreamed morosely of the Oldsmobile rotted away in one of them, of how the chassis would have been reduced by the tropical damp to a turquoise pool of rust. Or of how I'd arrive in Corozal to see it coming around the corner in a state of immaculate preservation.

But this wasn't a novel. I wasn't going to find Maria Julia, or Mr Kluivert, or Rasta Bob, or the rotting hulk of the Oldsmobile. I was prepared to find nothing at all.

But not prepared enough. Whatever I had expected, it was far worse. 'Corozal – we always call it the ghost town,' my landlady had told me in nearby Orange Walk. And I could see why.

There was bad weather heading into the bay and I remembered something my memory had blurred – that when I was here before, it had also been hurricane season, like now, and that my mood had fluctuated with the constant changes in the barometric pressure. Maybe that was why the streets were all deserted. Maybe that was why I felt a sudden gloom at being back. The only shop open was Payday Advances and Eazy Loans, 'where every day is payday'.

The old Miramar Hotel, where I'd hung my hat and communed with Roach, had gone, so rotten that it had just fallen down, according to the only taxi driver I could find in the main square. Roach had moved to Belmopan, and since died. No one remembered Mr Kluivert at all. The Don Quixote Hotel at Consejo, whose manager Max had advised torching the car to claim the insurance, had been replaced by a clinic for an American retirement complex. Even the fishing boats that used to line the docks had vanished, along with the fish, and with them the good-time girls, the brothels and the pool halls.

It was as if an eraser had wiped over the town. I arrived with black clouds hanging over the bay and by the time I had walked around the main square and talked to the taxi driver, it was clear that not one shred from my past visit remained. The rain broke in another heavy downpour.

I sheltered with the taxi driver, who was surprised to find anyone curious about Corozal. '*Nadie se detiene aquí*, nobody ever stops here,' he said quietly. '*Se van mas allá*, they go further on,' and he made that familiar gesture of unrolling a carpet ahead of him. It was good to hear Spanish being spoken again, after the English and Creole further south. But there was only so much of sitting with the taxi driver and looking at the rain that I could take. He drove me to the one place open for lunch, a run-down hotel just south of town, with a rotting jetty but no boat.

The rain stopped, and the sun came out on the still turbulent water of the completely empty bay. Looking at the sea reminded me of my friend Roger Deakin, who had once set out with an unusual mission: to swim across Britain by every means possible – starting with the small moat that surrounded his smallholding on a wild Suffolk moor and carrying on across rivers, estuaries, lakes and any water he came to; Roger had died of a sudden illness just the year before. I knew what he would have done here.

The hotel management refused to lend me a towel, although I promised to lunch there afterwards. Nor would they let me change or store my pack. It was ironic. After years of illicitly using hotel pools and getting away with it, now a hotel wouldn't let me swim in the open sea.

I stripped off anyway and jumped from the end of the hotel jetty, leaving my clothes and pack on the wooden planks. What were the hotel going to do – burn all my possessions while I swam out into the centre of the bay?

The water was not the clearest and there was debris swirling around my legs. Yet by the time I reached the centre of that wide expanse, and the land was just a thin blurred line, I felt cleansed and better. I lay on my back, floating, and looked at the clouds still whipping across the sky.

THE ISLANDS

L ooking out from the hotel restaurant, after fish soup and
several daiquiris, I could see that a ferry boat was getting ready
to sail from Corozal to the islands.

The islands. The idea awoke something long suppressed in me.
I had never reached the island Cayes off the Belize coast on my
first trip – how could I with two tons of metal and chassis tied to
my feet? – and yet they were meant to be the most idyllic part of
the country.

A friend had advised me to do on this return journey just what
I would have done at eighteen: 'Take off and be free,' she had said.
This presupposed, wrongly, that at eighteen I had felt free. I
remembered those Dylan lines from 'My Back Pages': 'I was so
much older then, I'm younger than that now.'

I was ready for the islands this time. And I had a sudden vision
of some barefoot travelling, light on my feet, with only an iPod
and some suncream; hadn't Jorge Luis Borges written a poem

complaining that his only regret at the end of a long life was not to have travelled lighter?

I liked the idea as well that this was where the Maya had come after abandoning their big inland cities – that they too had 'let go' after the environmental disaster of trying to clear the rainforests for agriculture, and instead lived a more seafaring life up and down these islands. Archaeologists had begun to find a surprising amount of evidence of late Maya occupation, particularly on the exotically named Ambergris Caye.

As we left Corozal behind, the captain of the small launch let me plug the iPod into the ship's speaker system so I could listen to Culture and 'Two Sevens Clash', the roots reggae of the late Seventies I had grown up with. Poking my head through the small bow-hatch, I let the wind blow me to pieces as the small mangrove islands peeled away to either side. Ahead lay the clear water inside the coral reef, the longest in the Western Hemisphere and one of the most unspoilt in the world; Charles Darwin had described it as 'the most remarkable reef in the West Indies'. The moment of anticipation was so perfect, I almost didn't want to arrive.

Caye Caulker (pronounced '*key cucker*') was not a dis-appointment: the launch docked at a pier just wide enough for the local boys to bicycle down in sweeping arcs; they could hang a tyre over the water for a tantalizing second before pulling it back. A strip of a town ran alongside the beach. The only three streets were called, with satisfying simplicity, Front Street, Middle Street and Back Street.

The north end of town was the best place to swim, by the channel called the Split that separated the island in half: it was where the kids and off-duty boatmen hung out. Over the nearby beach-bar, the Lazy Lizard, ran the legend, 'A sunny place for shady people'.

There was an old high diving board. As always, it felt even higher when you were standing on it; the wooden plank had a piratical springiness. Jumping off, I let the only partially salinated water force its way into my eyes as I sank deep; then the current drifted me back along the Split and out to sea, so that when I swam up onto the beach it was as if I had arrived from the mainland.

'Captain John' was barbecuing and selling shrimp sticks under a palm tree by the shore. I knew he was called Captain John because a little placard stuck in the sand told me so. He looked in his sixties, with a white and whiskery complexion; such an image of nautical mateyness that he could be selling Birds Eye Fish Fingers, were it not for his unexpected and graphic T-shirt, which said 'Shaven Beaver'. He told me that he had come down from Florida to retire, and sold the odd shrimp stick to make ends meet. But any idea that he had found ripe and mellow contentment was soon lost.

'I moved to get away from all those fucking Spanish in Florida. I was waiting in line at an election and this Spanish woman next to me had to have an interpreter to check which name she'd registered under. She had five IDs with her. Five. And I thought that's just enough. I mean if they want to be American, that's just part of the package. They could at least learn fucking English. So I moved here. How's the shrimp?'

Quite why he'd come to Belize, with its own high proportion of Spanish speakers, was unexplained. I moved on smartly, past the guesthouses with their hammocks stretched outside – some had slung hammocks on the jetties as well, presumably so you could fish during a siesta – the beach shacks renting out canoes and boats, and the small Chinese grocery stores. I was the only person who seemed to be walking in the sun rather than lying in the shade. A small crab gingerly crossed the sandy street with a balletic slowness and purpose.

Annie and Lionel 'Chocolate' Heredia were sitting out on their stoop. Annie had first come to the islands from New York in 1985 for a two-week diving trip and ended up staying over twenty years; she had married Chocolate, a now seventy-something Belizean, well known locally for his endless work trying to protect the sea cows of the reef, the manatees.

Annie told me how these gentle, large creatures grazed on sea grass in shallow waters and were as intelligent as dolphins, communicating with each other by wriggling their eyes. But the manatees were also easily hit in those same shallow waters by power boats, while their guts filled with the monofilament lines used by the fishermen. As a result, the manatee population in Belize had been reduced to a scant thousand.

She told me all this in something under a minute of greeting me from the chair on her stoop, speaking in a fast, staccato fashion, as people often do when they live close to a cause. Annie had short cropped hair and a firm gaze. I liked her, not least because she offered the use of a large room over their place to stay, and was impressed by Chocolate, who was dragging beach canoes around and looked wry and fit for a man of his age.

Together with Annie, Chocolate had set up a manatee sanctuary on a small island near Belize City called Swallow Caye. Rather than stripping out all the sea grass – commercial operators often depilated the seabed near beaches and reefs because it made for unattractive swimming – they had encouraged it. They also stopped spear-fishing boats from churning through the water with the propeller blades which could so easily rip into a manatee's flesh.

But now their sanctuary was under threat, for there were plans to build condominiums and docks on the neighbouring islands, with bridges between them and to the mainland that would disrupt the fragile sanctuary environment; these plans were largely the work of the cruise-ship operators.

Ever since I arrived in Belize, people had been telling me about the cruise operators. It was a problem that had only grown up in the last few years, as cut-price cruise ships had taken to sailing from Florida and Texas for a floating holiday around the Gulf of Mexico, disgorging their rubbish into the open seas and their passengers for day visits on shore.

The sheer scale of the operation was what caused concern. More than 800,000 cruise-ship visitors had landed during the past year – in a country of only around 250,000 inhabitants. No wonder the Belizeans felt swamped. And nor did *los cruceritos*, 'the little cruiser visitors', spend much money when they landed – an average of $45 each, nothing for a tourist, so the economy was not being helped. Moreover the *cruceritos* had gained a reputation in Belize for meanness and crass insensitivity, parachuting in for the day, buying the T-shirt – if that – and burning rubber to do a 'Maya Sites Trip' in a few hours before getting back to the mothership on time.

I had been amused to see this prospectus for a day tour of Belize City organised by Carnival, the biggest cruise-ship operator in Belize and indeed the world:

> *This excursion is one of the best ways to get a feel for magical Belize City. On this excursion you will:*
> - *Ride among the old wooden colonial homes and modern cement structures that line the narrow city streets of Belize*
> - *See landmarks such as the 200-year-old Cathedral and the famous lighthouse*
> - *Do some shopping in Belize City.*
> *Note: Restrooms are available at the House of Culture*

I signed Annie's petition against them. As with so many tropical paradises, I was beginning to gather that there was some grit in the coconut oil – and that relatively few of the inhabitants of Caye Caulker had been born on the island: many were travellers who had migrated there, including Belizeans who had found the mainland too intense.

But few had travelled quite as far as Obaidul and Mohammed, the quiet Bangladeshi friends who ran the Taj Indian Restaurant & Bar along the way. I had noticed it immediately as a rarity. It was the only restaurant selling Indian food I had seen in Belize – or for that matter in the whole of Latin America. Perhaps as a result, business was not good. The restaurant was empty and as the only customer I asked Obaidul and Mohammed how it was that two Bangladeshis had ended up on the other side of the world in Belize.

The afternoon rain came down and there was time to hear their story over some spiced bhindi bhaji and tikka masala, which the larger of the two, Mohammed, cooked for me as we talked. They had first gone to Germany, then to Mexico, but hadn't liked it, so had begun an odyssey through Central America, speaking no Spanish and attempting with increasing desperation to set up Indian restaurants in countries that had never heard of curry. After trying Cuba and Honduras, and finding it impossible to learn Spanish, they had settled in Belize City, which at least had the benefit of speaking English – but that had proved too violent, so they had moved here, to the islands. Obaidul looked out at the street, which was awash with water, and said in his soft, singsong voice, almost drowned out by the rain on the roof: 'We like it here. We can get our spices and grow okra.'

It felt wrong to ask them if the restaurant was a success – and because of the hurricanes, it was low season, so perhaps later in the year the tables would be packed with Belizeans forsaking their lobster and beans for a chicken madras.

*

Walking the streets again at dusk, after the rain had stopped, I could smell the barbecued fish and lobster from the simple shacks along the seashore, cooked with chillies and cumin. Reggae was pouring out of competing bars and restaurants. A few backpackers were swinging from their trees at the cheapest guesthouse in town, near the pier, where you dispensed with a room and just lived in a hammock.

I was drawn naturally to where the reggae was loudest, towards the south of town where most of the locals lived. It was coming from what looked like one of the tallest buildings on the island, all of three storeys. The club was called the 'I and I' and the entrance was up some side stairs beside the owner's house. I arrived at tree level into one of the wildest bars I had ever seen. The effect was like Swiss Family Robinson on skunk marijuana, a series of tree houses built out at crazy angles from the house into which the late-night crowds could swing as they wished, wandering out from the dark chill-out interiors into the treetops and back again.

The sound system was playing *Chant Down Babylon*, a series of mashed-up and mixed-up Bob Marley songs that had either been rapped or drum'n' bassed over, his sweet voice playing against the harsh rappers like the papaya and chilli sauce they served here with red snapper.

It was 'early hours' still and I seemed to be the only person in the club; I wandered from darkened room to darkened room and then into the tree houses, a cold Belikin beer in my hand. The music was so loud, I was holding onto the cold bottle for comfort. But right on the topmost level, with a view across the night-time city and a heron's angle down onto the game of pool being played at Marins bar below, I realised there was someone swinging off the hammocks slung from the rafters: a big local guy with Rasta locks and a T-shirt unable to contain his beer paunch. He was smoking a joint the size of a Pershing missile.

'Wa' some?' he asked. His voice was low and smoked, and I had to crane down towards him as he swung on the hammock.

'Wa' you lookin' for 'ere, mon?' he whispered.

I murmured in an English and self-deprecatory way that I wasn't quite sure.

'Tha's OK, mon. Tek your time. We all lookin' for the land of lost content, mon. The land of lost content.'

*

The next morning I looked out at dawn from my own balcony. At the end of the pier a bright-yellow sailing boat was being loaded with provisions. I noticed it immediately because this was an island largely of twin Yamaha-engined power boats, designed to get divers out on the sixty-mile trip to the Great Blue Hole at Lighthouse Reef. A sailing boat was an anachronism, but for me an appealing one.

Ever since a child, I had loved to sail, first on Suffolk estuaries like the Deben, later at Chew Valley Lake near the Mendips, where the south-westerlies whipped over the hills with a ferocious fillip and the birds gathered to shelter in the lee of Denny Island. Looking out at the sea, I could feel a breeze on my face.

The yellow boat was called *Ragga Gal* and was small and shallow-keeled, not much more than thirty feet in length.

'We're sailing later today, at ten. There's still a berth left. Three days to sail down south to Placencia.'

I had wandered out along the pier for a closer look and been button-holed by Amelia, the young girl in the hut that served as an office for the self-styled 'Raggamuffin crew'. As the last to join, I would be the seventh passenger, the only singleton with three couples. But more off-putting was the space. A 30-foot boat was never going to sleep seven of us, with a captain and his mate as well.

'We sleep on the islands – English Caye, or Rendezvous Caye, or Tobacco Caye. It depends on the wind. The captain says there's a northerly rising.'

I turned to face the wind on the pier. The lightest of sprays was flicking off the waves onto my face. Amelia was reeling me in. The names of the Cayes were those that had been given to them by the early English privateers and pirates (not that there was much difference). They had made this coast their own, with its ferocious reef and small islands where men could hide from both the Spanish and the English authorities.

I didn't even know where Placencia was. But it sounded a good place to sail to.

The captain was a tall Nicaraguan, with a darker skin than many Belizeans, and a commanding physical presence. The first thing he did was to ask everyone to put their shoes in a bag that was stowed away for the duration. 'This is a barefoot boat. That's rule one. And for this trip I have decided to call myself Miguel. That's not my real name but it's a name I've always wanted to have.'

I had never met a captain of a small boat who didn't have attitude. And Miguel – for that was indeed his real name – had plenty.

His mate Dice was a local, younger, quieter and smaller, but equally good looking. As I found out in the ensuing days, he was a romantic who claimed to be recovering from a sequence of heartless but beautiful girls who had been travelling through the cayes.

And so began a magical period of time out of time as we sailed south. Miguel was an excellent free diver, as he told us, and not shy about showing off his abilities. He took us snorkelling in fabulous reefs that were too far from Caulker to be used by the day-trippers, let alone the cruise ships, which could only penetrate the coral reef by the few deep-water channels leading to Belize City.

With his spear gun loaded – largely for show – he would sink deep below the wall of the coral and then, just when it seemed he must surely come up for air, go yet further down to flush something out. On several occasions he disturbed conger eel from their hiding places; one turned and gave a sharp inquisitive look straight at me, with its malevolent, snake-like head.

I had snorkelled before, off Bonaire in the Dutch Antilles, which has some of the best walk-in snorkelling in the world. But this was altogether more satisfying, slipping from the side of a sailing boat into some nameless section of the reef and seeing one's fellow passengers transformed into weightless and floating mer-folk swimming with the fishes.

And what fishes: large shoals of blue tang floating over and around the elkhorn coral; yellow snapper and the striped school-master fish; Nassau groupers and the odd pork fish as loners within the group; a peacock flounder near the bottom. And then the stingrays, swimming in majesty and leisure, or burrowing down into the sand, the best possible reason never to rest your flipper on the seabed if you could possibly help it.

At one point I felt someone swimming along beside me and

turned to see which member of the group it might be, only to find a spotted eagle ray calmly keeping pace at almost arm's length, the largest of the stingrays after the manta.

Much of the reef was still healthy compared to some of the deterioration that coral had experienced worldwide as sea temperatures rose. But there was still a sense of elegy, a feeling that if I returned in ten, twenty, let alone another thirty years time I might not be able to see delicate blue damselfish nibbling around the polyps, the fan coral waving in the current or the squiggles of brain coral clustered on the bottom.

Once we came upon a manatee sleeping on the sea floor, as these gentle creatures tend to for much of the time. Miguel lay beside it without getting close enough to touch – not of course what you should do, but it was oddly moving to see human lying beside sea cow on the ocean bed, both prostrate and protected by the waters above them. The bulk of the manatee dwarfed Miguel.

Later I saw the manatee swimming past with surprising speed: they can get up to speeds of 20 miles an hour; its one large tail flipper was undulating up and down in powerful waves before it disappeared into the blue and towards the breakers of the reef.

*

We saw English Caye from afar, a dot on the Caribbean. It was a cartoon island, with a few palms, a lighthouse and a jetty, surrounded by a coral reef. It even had an abandoned sailor – the sole inhabitant, who it turned out had been living there for the last thirty years and had raised a now departed family on the tiny island while being titular guardian of the lighthouse.

The first thing I did, for the symmetry of it, was to swim right around the island – not as easy as it looked, as finding a way through the coral labyrinth was complicated and I was mindful of Miguel's injunction to avoid touching the coral at all costs. There were clouds of tiny fish to pass through and branches of antler coral.

We put up tents under the palms and ate out on the jetty – a grouper cooked by Miguel in a coconut sauce and some lobster *ceviche* prepared by Dice, washed down with rum punch. I found that drinking rum here was like vodka in Russia – you were given so much in a constant drip feed that you soon stopped noticing. We sat out late, putting the world to rights, helped by the rum and the roots reggae.

By now there had been time enough and more to get to know my fellow passengers: Michael was a burly Californian surfer who worked as a fireman so he could take advantage of the shift system for long leaves of absence on the waves; his actress girlfriend Anneka, who said of the fire department that it was 'boy heaven' in that all the firemen were moonlighting physical fitness enthusiasts; Bram and Karen, a young Belgian couple, who like many others I had met from that country were adventurous and inquisitive; Ollie from Germany and Annie from Grenoble, who had met on a previous journey to Bolivia, now lived together in France, but conversed eccentrically in Spanish as the best *lingua franca* between them.

It was exactly the sort of group I liked on my travels, self-selecting in that only a certain sort of traveller was likely to head off on a barefoot journey in a tiny boat, adventurous and full of engaging stories. That said, after a few rum punches before the mast in the sun and a day spent snorkelling, I'd have felt warm and companionable with Saddam Hussein or Adolf Eichmann.

We spaced ourselves across the island, each camping under one of the palms. I woke in the middle of night and wandered out to see the lighthouse flashing above me, looking with its giant eye like one of the Martians from *The War of the Worlds*. In the sky were the familiar constellations of Orion and Gemini, with the dog star winking below and Venus on the horizon.

And out at sea was a bizarre apparition: a cruise ship had arrived during the night and moored in the deep channel that led to Belize City, presumably in order to disgorge its day-trip passengers the next day. It was lit up like a candelabra, an absurd vision of a carnival (and it was a Carnival Cruise Line ship) as well as of over-consumption, like an office tower block at night with all the lights still on.

I hunkered down on the water's edge to watch it, feeling the cool breeze that was keeping away the mosquitoes and having an unusual urge for a cigarette. I had given up a long time ago and the memory of being an eighteen-year-old who couldn't get through the day without a Marlboro was a far-off one.

What with the lighthouse, the stars and the blazing cruise ship, the sand was lit up like a stage and the water was as dark as an audience. I suddenly felt unusually close to my other eighteen-year-old self. What would he have said if he had stayed in Belize and, like the lighthouse keeper, spent the last thirty years in isolation on this island, to then see me arrive? Surprise that I still had most of my hair? My petrol emotion now certainly ran at a steadier pace than then, with fewer dreams and solar flares but maybe more achievements and results. He would have disapproved deeply of the idea of divorce, like most people who have never experienced it. He would be saddened at the news of those close friends of mine who had died. And he would have been horrified that I now liked Neil Young.

But he might have been surprised at the extent to which I was still searching. We often assume as teenagers that adulthood and maturity await, even serenity – that after a necessary period of transition, round the corner will come the perfect partner, job and life. But the period of transition can last, or reoccur, until the day you die. And the urge to keep travelling, at least for me, was as constant as ever.

*

The sailing was easy in some ways, because the reef protected the coastal waters from the full force of the waves, but more difficult in others, in that the coral formations were often close to the surface and made navigation complicated, even with our small shallow-keeled boat. That shallow keel caused *Ragga Gal* to drift with any side winds; moreover, the sail didn't fit either the boom or the mast as Dice told me the sail-makers had sent the wrong one. But Miguel helmed with aplomb, moving the tiller with one leg as he fished behind the boat. I looked up at one point to see a large grouper hooked and bouncing over the waves towards us across our own wake; Miguel gutted it with a few quick slits of the knife and tossed the fish into a bucket, all while steering.

I could see why this whole area had been a pirates' playground: the archipelago of sheltered, tiny islands with evocative names like Blackadore Caye, the local knowledge needed to find your way through the channels and the deep-water port at Belize City if you needed to repair your boat. Privateers like Morgan, Drake and Hawkins were in a perfect position to ambush the Spanish treasure galleons as they sailed from Honduras or Panama in the south, laden with the gold that would enable Charles V and his successors to prosecute their European wars – hence the tacit encouragement of these '*piratas*' by the British authorities.

The very name 'Belize' was said to be not a local one but to come from the Spanish pronunciation of Peter 'Wallace', a Scottish freebooting pirate and old lieutenant of Sir Walter Raleigh, who had established the first more permanent settlement on the coast in 1638. And while Columbus had named the island that controlled access to the deep-water channel 'Punta Caxinas', the pirates had renamed it 'St George's Caye' in a quixotic spirit of patriotism, given their ambivalent relationship to the crown. Other islands had similar redolent names: Gallows Point Reef, Sergeant's Caye, Frenchman's Caye, Spanish Lookout Caye, North Drowned Caye and several named after individual pirates, Ramsey's Caye, Grennel's Caye and Simmonds Caye.

In recent years academics had changed their views on these pirates of the Caribbean. Rather than the glamorous, freebooting rockstars of the myths and the movies, they were now seen more as working-class heroes (and gender or race heroes if blacks or women, as a few of them were) who had escaped an authoritarian society to set up attractively free-thinking and cooperative communities.

The pirates who settled on the Belizean mainland began to export the lucrative logwood and mahogany, greatly to the irritation of the Spaniards who controlled all the surrounding territories. In 1629, Philip IV of Spain set up a coast guard to try to control pirate activity off Belize, but to little avail.

St George's Caye was the scene of a critical battle in 1798 when a handful of English settlers and 'baymen' saw off a Spanish fleet and established the country as a British colony; despite this, Guatemala continued to the present day to claim the territory as its own – one reason why Belize had been the last British colony in the Americas to gain its independence, and why the British Army was still a protective presence in the country.

That spirit of a scavenging, piratical community still lived on.

During the Second World War local fishermen from Caye Caulker had collected the floating cargo from torpedoed ships in the Caribbean, the most lucrative catch being bales of rubber. And the islands still made great places to transfer smuggled cargo, whether it be to evade duty or drugs charges.

The hours rolled by as I lay back and watched a *frigata magnificens*, 'magnificent frigate bird', circling high overhead, while our loose-fitting sail flapped and pulled to the top of the stepped mast. What with the sun, the reggae and the rum, after a while the islands all started to look the same – God knows how the pirates had remembered where they had left that buried treasure.

We arrived at Rendezvous Caye, one of the islands used by the pirates: it was the smallest we had yet landed on, less than the size of a football pitch and with a perfect spun-sand beach to every side. We landed and were beginning to enjoy a swim in some of the purest waters I had ever experienced, when a large tender arrived from the cruise ship, spilling out music and loud-mouthed passengers.

Unlike *Ragga Gal*, whose shallow keel allowed it to glide right onto the beach, the tender had to moor offshore, and we faced off against them, like native Indians watching the Spaniards arrive. The cruise passengers eyed the water, as if contemplating an amphibious invasion across the short stretch that separated them from the beach. But the captain announced on his Tannoy that they would only be there for ten minutes, 'SO STAY ON THE BOAT!', before departing, the thrash of their engines amplifying the bass of the music across the water as the tender receded into the distance with great speed.

As I swam into the again peaceful waters, needle fish started to jump past me out of the waves and there was the looming, barrelled shape of a barracuda where the sand ramped down to the sea.

I had an old surfer's rash vest, necessary given the amount of time our fair European skins were spending in the water; while drying it on deck I often chatted with Dice, who liked coming in front of the mast while Miguel helmed, not least to get away from his captain's stern orders or Captain Ahab moods.

Dice was about twenty-five and had grown up in the country with his Adventist parents before training to be an engineer in Belize City. But like the 'country boy / and no one knows your name' the Heptones had sung about, Dice had got lost in the city: 'I couldn't take the aggravation, so one day I just took the last ferry out to the islands – and I knew when I was doing it that I was never coming back. And I didn't.' He had got a job as a boat builder, specialising in tailoring transoms for the ever more powerful outboard motors that their owners demanded. Then he had moved to the more relaxed Ragamuffin world of sailing down the reef, for him the perfect job – and one I would have loved myself at that age, if I hadn't been chasing the chimera of film and fortune around the world.

Dice said he was not in the mood for 'bad vibes' from Miguel because he had slept badly the previous night. I asked Dice if he was married and he said no, but he had a three-year-old daughter living with her mother in the country; the mother got pregnant without warning him and 'shattered his heart so bad you could strain it back through a hole'.

Now he was thinking of joining the British Army, who were actively recruiting Belizeans. I tried to dissuade him; the thought of Dice going to fight in Afghanistan was not a good one. It emerged that one reason for his interest was a past romantic attachment to a female soldier stationed in Belize. I was reminded of the vulnerability and occasional naivety of young men, and of course of my own.

*

I woke early in my beautiful room on Tobacco Caye, in a lodging house called Reef End: a place as simple as its name, with just four bedrooms built up on stilts round a tiny bay where *Ragga Gal* was moored. A small black cat was looking up at me. My room had windows on three sides; there were no curtains, so the dawn sun came through like whitewash. There was a hammock on the veranda and conch shells up the stairs. I had a hangover as the rum was starting to catch up with me, but I had a clear vision of the night before.

I had settled in at the small bar on the island with an older man, a Texan who was passing through. I never learnt his name. He had a weather-beaten face like a roll-up, and a shirt that looked as if he'd run over a fruit in the water.

Two pretty girls from another boat who were walking by had been his cue to open a conversation: 'Wouldn't you like just to lift up those cute little skirts?', said the Texan. It seemed a purely rhetorical question, so I let it ride.

His hair was wild and unkempt from the salt spray and the speed he'd been travelling at. We started talking about his boat, one of the most powerful I had seen on the island, and he persuaded me to join him drinking Green Stripe, a mixture of rum with peppermint and aniseed that tasted like the strong medicine it was.

'Those are twin Yamaha F350 V8s, each with a 5.3 litre engine. Designed my own transom to take them – and those are the best four-stroke, computer-controlled, fuel-injected engines on the market, with variable camshaft timing, multiple valves and super-charging.' I had no idea what he was talking about, but even I could tell it was a powerful boat.

'The best motor you can have. And in these islands you can hide anywhere. Or go anywhere. You want to run stuff over to 'Duras or Nicaragua, no one's going to know. And I don't mean drugs or any of that shit. There's plenty of other possibilities round here. Business possibilities.'

He took a deep hit of his Green Stripe. And then he closed.

'You should buy yourself a boat, a boat you could live on. Be your own agent. Then you could sail anywhere you want, in the world. You know. And stow what you want, and go anywhere.'

'You can buy mine if you want. It's on the market.' It was the sell.

He swigged again at his Green Stripe and made a wave of his hand to the ocean, as if unrolling a carpet. It was a gesture I remembered well. For the world was always full of infinite possibilities. Even if you didn't always take them.

ACKNOWLEDGEMENTS

I would like to thank: Jim Aimers, Angus Brodnax Bell, Fiona Cadwallader, John Elliott, Adriana Diaz Enciso, Amy Finger, Elizabeth Graham, David Huerta, Barry Isaacson, Nicola Keane, Irena Postlova, James Pursey, Janette Scott, Laurie Gwen Shapiro, Alex Tait, Benedict Taylor, Gary Ziegler; my extended family for their support both 'then' and 'now'; my agent Georgina Capel and the editorial team of Francine Brody, Bea Hemming and Alan Samson at Weidenfeld & Nicolson; and every Mexican who ever bought me a drink.

HIGHLY SELECTIVE BIBLIOGRAPHY

John Reed's *Insurgent Mexico* was published in 1914, but does not include all his original reports from the Mexican front for American periodicals like *Metropolitan Magazine* and *The World*.

The longer story of Pancho Villa and the Mexican Revolution is told by Frank McLynn in *Villa and Zapata* (2001). His widow Luz Villa's *Pancho Villa en la Intimidad* ('An Intimate Portrait of Pancho Villa') of 1976 is harder to obtain.

Cortés's *Five Letters to the Emperor Charles V* remain the most vivid account of both the Spanish Conquest and the man. The full history of *The Conquest of Mexico* is related by first Prescott (1843) and then Hugh Thomas (1993), while the Mexican historian Miguel León-Portilla has investigated the sinister figure of Tlacaelel and Náhuatl reactions to the invaders in his *Visión de los Vencidos* (*The Broken Spears*) of 1959 and many other books.

In 1927, D. H. Lawrence followed his novel *The Plumed Serpent* with the travel book *Mornings in Mexico*; likewise, Graham Greene paired *The Power and The Glory* with *The Lawless Roads* (1940, 1939); Evelyn Waugh published *Robbery Under Law: The Mexican Object-Lesson* in 1939; and Aldous Huxley his *Beyond the Mexique Bay* in 1934. Huxley then used Mexico as a location for *Eyeless in Gaza* (1936).

Malcolm Lowry's *Under the Volcano* appeared in 1947, almost ten years after the autobiographical events they describe. His

ex-wife Jan Gabrial wrote a memoir about their stay in Cuernavaca, the aptly titled *Inside the Volcano* (2001). I was also wrong
at the time to suppose that no one else was interested in Lowry's
passion for golf: see 'Real and imaginary golf-course systems of
order in Malcolm Lowry's *Under the Volcano*', a PhD thesis by
D. J. Hadfield, University of Warwick, 1982.

Robert Lowell's poems on Mexico were first published in
Notebook (1969) and then rewritten *For Lizzie and Harriet* (1973).

The story of how the glyphs were finally translated has been
well told by Michael Coe in *Breaking the Maya Code* (1992, revised
1999), perhaps the only book on linguistics that can be deemed
an exciting page-turner. His book on *The Maya* (which with all
the recent revelations has needed to be heavily revised for every
edition over the years since its first publication in 1966) is authori-
tative, as is David Drew's *The Lost Chronicles of the Maya Kings*
(1999). James J. Aimers's essay 'What Maya Collapse? Terminal
Classic Variation in the Maya Lowlands', in the *Journal of Archaeological Research* 15, 329 (2007), questions received wisdom on what
happened to the Maya.

Marcus Rediker has written about the Caribbean pirates in
Between the Devil and the Deep Blue Sea (1993) and *Villains of All
Nations* (2004).

The Owner's Handbook for the Oldsmobile 98, 1972 model,
is sometimes available on eBay.

INDEX